FOOD
+
BEER

Ross Dobson

FOOD + BEER

Great food to eat with beer

MURDOCH BOOKS

CONTENTS

FOOD + BEER = HAPPINESS

F
+
B

> He was a wise man who invented beer.
> — Folk proverb

There is more than a little truth in the suggestion that beer is mankind's greatest ever invention.

The agricultural revolution was thought to be all about food — but in recent times, some scientific anthropological-type folks have suggested that man/woman actually cultivated the first barley crops not to make bread, but to make beer. It was this thirsty appetite that motivated people to grow the grains needed to make beer; bread was more an afterthought. It's reassuring to know that our ancestors had their priorities right.

This universally common interest in and desire for beer could explain why beer has been a part of many cultures, world over, well before such geographically separate groups of people had contact with one another.

In times long ago, beer ticked all the boxes: it was easy to make; it was safe to drink; and back in the day when we were not so obsessed about our weight, beer contained all-important calories, imperative for refuelling the body after a day of exhausting physical labour.

> For a quart of ale is a dish for a king.
> — William Shakespeare

It is now thought that some beer was being brewed as far back as 9000 years ago, and that the oldest recorded written recipe is for beer. So, someone made beer and it was enjoyed so much that they chiselled the recipe onto a piece of stone to preserve for all time. It sounds positively Flintstone-esque, but this is not cartoon fiction, folks — the invention of beer is an elementary part of our evolution.

Earlier beers were made with cereal grains such

as barley and wheat; the addition of hops, which is such a distinguishing feature of modern beers, came much later. Hops gives brews a more complex, bitter flavour, as well as being a natural preservative.

(On a side note, in biology things are classified into groups or families. Hops is from the same family as cannabis. That's one very happy family!)

> Never underestimate how much assistance, how much satisfaction, how much comfort, how much soul and transcendence there might be in a well-made taco and a cold bottle of beer.
> — Tom Robbins, author

Research suggests that the taste of beer alone is enough to trigger the release of a pleasure chemical in the brain. And this is an instant good feeling that has nothing to do with the intoxicating effects of beer. That is, the taste of the beer alone, without any intoxicating effect from the alcohol,

triggers activity in the brain's reward centres. It is the same for eating: something tastes good to us and we enjoy eating it. Put food and beer together in one room and you have a pleasurable combo indeed.

> In wine there is wisdom.
> In beer there is freedom.
> In water there is bacteria.
> — Proverb

After water and tea, beer is the world's third most consumed drink, and the most widely consumed alcoholic drink. Think about this for a moment. Water… well, it's just there, isn't it? And tea is the dried leaf of a plant that really only needs to be dunked in boiling water. But beer is something else. Its preparation requires planning and crafting.

In many countries the marketing of beer is clearly aimed at a target audience: men. History and sexism play a hand here. Many women were not permitted to drink alcohol in the same places as men. If they were, it was often in a separate room with limited choices of drink — think sherry, cherry

F + B

brandy or shandy (beer diluted with lemonade) in the ladies' lounge or hotel parlour room. Many drinking institutions, such as pubs and hotels, would close in the early evening. This would allow men to drink after work, but left no time for women to enjoy a beer — they were at home making sure a lovely plate of food was ready on the table when the pub had closed!

After World War II, however, the baby boomers called for change. The concept of the teenager evolved. Women started drinking whatever they wanted, and in the same places as men. The fairer sex like beer too, you know.

> Give me a woman who loves beer and I will conquer the world.
> — Kaiser Wilhelm, German emperor

Beer is one of life's pleasures, and the idea of enjoying food and booze together is by no means novel. What we prefer to drink with food is influenced by convention, as well as the ingredients themselves. When it comes to wine, there are only two choices, right? Red or white. The basic rule of eating chicken and seafood with white wine, and eating red meat and rich, creamy dishes with red wine, is very much an old-world notion, even though there is much credit in these pairings.

Arguably, however, beer may well be a better drink to pair with food than wine. There is certainly more variety of ingredients: beer can be made with the inclusion of barley, hops, yeast as well as rice and spices. The resulting flavours are complex and layered, leaving greater options to match with the flavours in food, especially dishes containing herbs and citrus.

> Beer: it's the best damn drink in the world.
> — Jack Nicholson, actor

These orthodox notions of pairing wine and food were probably a class thing. Simply put, rich people ate at restaurants, or in castles or wherever else poor people didn't eat. Dining out was considered a privilege — at least by the underclass who never ate at restaurants — and etiquette and decorum dictated behaviour at the dining table. Fashion, food, drink fads and fancies often began at the top of the social order and trickled down, if at all.

> Beer is proof that God loves us and wants us to be happy.
> — Proverb

Beer really had no place in the restaurants of by-gone eras, as food was meant to be enjoyed with wine. Beer was something the working-class man drank with his meat-and-two-veg dinner or at a football game.

But the rise of the middle class changed all that. Now many of us are savvy enough to know what we want to drink with our food. The phenomena of the celebrity chef and the cooking show — not to mention the cookery book and the internet — means we are exposed to food and ingredients like never before.

Supermarkets juggle exotic ingredients on the shelf, depending on what is the 'flavour of the month'.

Table salt has been replaced by sea salt, tomato sauce by sweet chilli sauce, evaporated milk by coconut milk, and old-school dried herbs like basil (does anyone actually use this?) are now overlooked in favour of fresh and fragrant Thai basil, lemongrass or kaffir lime. And so it goes.

We have become a savvy, hungry bunch of consumers who know what it is we want to eat and what we want to drink. Things have moved a long way from the question, 'Would you like white or red?' The restaurant sommelier must now possess a broad and deep knowledge of beer as well.

> There is always something happening around a beer.
> — Alfred Heineken

Discount air travel allows us to travel more frequently and further than ever before in our history. Like fine dining, air travel is no longer the exclusive preserve of the rich and famous. Travel allows us to see, touch, smell and taste food from afar. There is so much less palaver, paperwork and preparation for international travel —

these days, the biggest travel decision we need to make is which search engine to use to book hotels and restaurants halfway across the world.

> You can't be a real country unless you have a beer and an airline. It helps if you have some kind of a football team, or some nuclear weapons, but at the very least you need a beer.
> — Frank Zappa, musician

Whether it be pizza after a sports game in the United States, roadside curry in India, chilli-spiked chicken in an Indonesian warung, a golden fried schnitzel, rösti or goulash in the heart of Europe, rest assured there will be a local beer to wash it all down. Generally speaking, it will be a local beer that goes with the local food. It is an interdependent relationship of sorts. If it were in nature, we would call it symbiotic.

I'm not saying don't drink wine, of course. Wine is a much better partner with some acidic foods, especially tomato-based sauces with pasta, and some dishes heavy in dairy cream. But nothing really cuts through salty, fried, fatty foods like the bubbly fresh fizz of a cold beer. The carbonation cleanses the palate after a bite of deep-fried squid. The coldness will feel good against hot food. It just feels like the right thing to be drinking.

> Not all chemicals are bad. Without chemicals such as hydrogen and oxygen, for example, there would be no way to make water, a vital ingredient in beer.
> — Dave Barry, author

Beer has been around for so long, one could ask if it has influenced what food is best enjoyed with beer. I mean, you don't really think of drinking stout or Guinness with sushi, or Thai fried rice dishes containing crab. If you love pale ale, you'll probably like it with anything you eat. And there's nothing wrong with that. There are no 'wrong' answers or hard-and-fast rules when pairing food with beer, or vice versa, although some combinations work better than others.

I'm thinking of the classic recipe for red braising in

Chinese cookery — where chicken, beef or pork are slowly poached in a savoury, sweet and fragrant pool of soy sauce, rice wine, star anise and cinnamon. Here the unctuous meat and flavourings are best paired with a stout or fruity wheat beer.

On the other hand, thin slices of red braised pork belly stir-fried with ginger, garlic and chilli, or red braised chicken deep-fried and served with a five-spice dipping salt... well, now we're ready for a pilsener or lager.

This book is for all of you (and you know exactly who you are) who have experienced pleasure in the company of food and beer.

Cheers!

1

KICKING OFF

I'm thinking weekend, I'm thinking holidays and I'm thinking sun. But then again, I'm also thinking homemade, spiced beer nuts with a cleansing ale by the fire. And doesn't that say a great deal about the versatility of beer?

Kick off the evening's proceedings with any of the 'social food' in this chapter. This is chatting, grazing and mingling food. Anytime food. Snacks and more-ish fried morsels, flavoured with chilli, salty soy, tangy vinegars and citrus. This is food to serve casually, with just a few napkins. And, as it's just to get things going, you probably don't want anything too aggressive to drink — maybe a crisp lager or a hoppy brew with a touch of spice and bitterness.

BEER NUTS

I've used peanuts here, but I've also been making this for years using raw almonds. This recipe is a really great little number to get the palate going and the tongues wagging about your culinary skills at the start of the evening. No one would believe how easy beer nuts are to make, so let's not spoil the illusion. And don't let my opinions sway you: any beer will go just fine with beer nuts.

500 g *(1 lb 2 oz)* **raw peanuts** > *skin on*

1 tablespoon **Spanish smoked paprika**

1 teaspoon **dried thyme**

1 teapoon **chilli flakes**

1 teaspoon **sea salt**

1 tablespoon **soft brown sugar**

2 tablespoons **olive oil**

SERVES
4

1 · · · Preheat the oven to 180°C (350°F). Line a baking tray with baking paper and put the peanuts in a bowl.

2 · · · Combine the paprika, thyme, chilli, salt, sugar and oil to make a paste. Add to the peanuts and stir with a large metal spoon to coat them evenly.

3 · · · Tumble the nuts onto the baking tray, spreading them out evenly. Transfer to the oven and roast for 7–8 minutes, or until darkened and aromatic. Shake the tray and stir well, then roast for another 4–5 minutes.

4 · · · Remove from the oven and leave to cool before serving. The beer nuts will keep in an airtight container for several days.

ONION BHAJI

I'm sure many of us don't deep-fry much at home. So, if you're going to bring out the deep-fryer, why not set some time aside and cook up a couple of dishes? This bhaji and the pakora opposite are two really authentic and simple Indian recipes that can be prepared together. Of course, you don't have to make both. Each one is a perfectly more-ish treat on its own, especially with a refreshing lager.

110 g *(3¾ oz/1 cup)* **besan** *(chickpea flour)*

1 tablespoon **rice flour**

1 teaspoon **fennel seeds**

1 teaspoon **cumin seeds**

12 **small curry leaves**

1 **large red chilli** > *thinly sliced*

1 tablespoon **lemon juice**

25 g *(1 oz/½ cup)* **finely chopped coriander** *(cilantro)*

1 **large onion** > *thinly sliced*

1 **onion** > *roughly grated*

vegetable oil > *for frying*

plain yoghurt, sweet mango chutney and lemon wedges > *to serve*

MAKES **8**

1 ··· **Put the besan, rice flour, fennel, cumin, curry leaves and chilli in a bowl and stir well.**

2 ··· **Add the lemon juice to 185 ml (6 fl oz/¾ cup) cold water. Add to the flour mixture and beat with a fork until lump-free. Stir in the coriander and the sliced and grated onions, separating any onion slices that are stuck together.**

3 ··· **Pour about 2 cm (¾ inch) vegetable oil into a non-stick frying pan. Heat the oil over high heat until shimmering. Use metal tongs to roughly measure out about ¼ cup of the onion mixture into the hot oil.**

4 ··· **Repeat to make four bhaji and cook in the oil for 6–8 minutes, turning often, until golden and crisp. Drain on paper towel while you allow the oil to reheat, then fry another four bhaji. Serve with yoghurt, chutney and lemon wedges.**

GREEN CHILLI PAKORA

I ate something like these in a very old-school Indian restaurant in London. It wasn't a 'high street' restaurant — it was in the heart of the West End, up several flights of stairs. And the Kingfisher lagers they were serving were 'long necks' (Aussie slang for 750 ml/26 fl oz bottles).

110 g *(3¾ oz/1 cup)* **besan** *(chickpea flour)*
¼ teaspoon **sea salt**
¼ teaspoon **chilli powder**
vegetable oil > *for frying*
8 **large green chillies**
lemon wedges and sea salt > *to serve*

MAKES **12**

1 · · · Combine the besan, salt and chilli powder in a bowl. Add 170 ml (5½ fl oz/⅔ cup) cold water and whisk to make a smooth batter.

2 · · · Pour about 2 cm (¾ inch) vegetable oil into a non-stick frying pan. Heat the oil over high heat. When the surface of the oil is shimmering, dip half the chillies in the batter, making sure they are coated all over.

3 · · · Lower the battered chillies into the hot oil and cook for 6–8 minutes, turning them often using metal tongs, until the batter forms a golden and slightly puffed crust around the chillies. Drain on paper towel while you cook the rest. Serve with lemon and sea salt.

ONION BHAJI & GREEN CHILLI PAKORA

SHREDDED DUCK PANCAKES

This is a fabulous at-home version of Peking duck pancakes. There is an awful lot of palaver involved in making authentic Peking duck at home. So, after going to a northern Chinese restaurant where slow-cooked shredded duck meat was served, I realised there was more than one way to skin a cat. Or cook a duck. Serve with Tsingtao or any crisp and light lager — the cool crunch of the cucumber here deserves a cool, crisp brew.

MAKES **12**

60 ml *(2 fl oz/¼ cup)* **dark soy sauce**

1 tablespoon **soft brown sugar**

2 **spring onions** *(scallions)* > *cut into 3–4 cm (1¼–1½ inch) lengths*

3 **garlic cloves** > *crushed*

5 thin slices **fresh ginger**

2 **star anise**

1 **cinnamon stick**

2 **duck breast fillets** > *skin on*

12 **ready-made Peking duck pancakes** > *from Asian food stores*

hoisin sauce, cucumber batons and spring onion *(scallion)* **batons** > *to serve*

1 · · · **Preheat the oven to 150°C (300°F). Put the soy sauce, sugar, spring onion, garlic, ginger, star anise and cinnamon in a small ceramic baking dish or ovenproof saucepan.**

2 · · · **Sit the duck breasts in the dish, cover tightly with foil and bake for 3 hours. The duck meat should be fork-tender and easy to shred.**

3 · · · **Reserving the braising liquid, peel the skin off each duck breast, in one piece. Place the duck skin on a baking tray lined with baking paper. Increase the oven temperature to 240°C (475°F) and roast the skin for about 10 minutes, or until dark and crisp. Allow the skin to cool, then break or slice into thin strips.**

4 · · · **Put the duck breast meat in a bowl with 60 ml (2 fl oz/¼ cup) of the reserved braising liquid. Using two forks, finely shred the meat onto a serving plate.**

5 · · · **To serve, take the pancakes and spread some hoisin sauce on each. Top with shredded duck, some cucumber and spring onion, then wrap the pancakes up. Serve with the crispy duck skin strips.**

TEX MEX SALAD

KICKING OFF

No place does Tex Mex quite like California and the south-western states of the USA. I ate this salad at someone's house — it was just a simple thing they liked to 'throw together' for last-minute barbecues. It seems to feature all the good bits of nachos thrown into a salad, but is better for you... not that this is usually an issue on 'beer night'! I like a pale lager with this one.

SERVES **4**

250 g *(9 oz)* **white corn tortillas** > *cut into very thin strips*

½ **iceberg lettuce** > *shredded*

2 **ripe tomatoes** > *cut into thin wedges*

1 **firm avocado** > *flesh cut into wedges*

1 **red onion** > *thinly sliced*

large handful **coriander** *(cilantro)* **sprigs**

handful **Spanish olives**

50 g *(1¾ oz/⅓ cup)* **crumbled firm feta cheese**

25 g *(1 oz/¼ cup)* **shaved parmesan cheese**

lime wedges > *to serve*

1 ··· Just before serving, put the tortilla strips in a large bowl. Add the lettuce, tomatoes, avocado, onion, coriander and olives.

2 ··· Use your hands or tongs to gently toss the salad together — you don't want to mush things up too much. Sprinkle with the combined cheeses and freshly ground black pepper. Serve with lime wedges.

TARAMASALATA

'Tarama' means mullet roe, 'salata' means salad… and the salty creaminess of this much-loved dip really gets the tastebuds going. If you want to make an authentic version, you must pay close attention to the very few ingredients required here. Use a decent loaf of bread — stale is fine, but not processed white. And you simply must use mullet roe: nothing else will do. Pair it with a pale ale.

SERVES

4

8 thick slices **stale white bread** > *crusts removed*

1 **onion** > *very finely grated*

2 **garlic cloves**

3 tablespoons **mullet roe** *(tarama)*

185 ml *(6 fl oz/¾ cup)* **light olive oil**

2 tablespoons **lemon juice**

warm pita bread and olives > *to serve*

1 · · · **Put the bread in a bowl and cover with cold water. Leave for a few minutes, then tip into a colander over the sink. Squeeze out as much water as you can, leaving about 2 cups of soggy bread.**

2 · · · **Put the bread in a food processor with the onion, garlic and mullet roe, then process until well combined. In a slow and steady stream, add the oil until the mixture resembles pink whipped cream.**

3 · · · **Add the lemon juice and a pinch of sea salt. Refrigerate until needed; the dip will thicken during chilling. Serve with warm pita bread and olives.**

GUACAMOLE

A good guacamole should not look like green ice cream, or be smooth, homogenous or processed-looking. Think 'chunky' without 'mushy'. The amount of onion may intrigue and you might think it will dominate the subtle avocado, but I find it adds a crisp freshness. Don't drink anything too heavy here. It would be easy to go with the flow and have a light, weak Mexican beer with a wedge of lemon but, for want of a better word: don't. American pale ale would be my choice.

2 **large ripe avocados** > *flesh cut into bite-sized chunks*	
1 **small white onion** > *very finely chopped*	
1 **jalapeño chilli** > *seeded and very finely chopped*	
½ teaspoon **sea salt**	
1 tablespoon **lime juice**	
10 g *(¼ oz/¼ cup)* **roughly chopped coriander** *(cilantro)*	
white corn chips > *to serve*	

SERVES 4

1 · · · Put the avocado in a large serving bowl. Combine the onion, chilli, salt and lime juice, then add to the avocado. Add the coriander and gently stir so the avocado is well coated in the other ingredients, but not mushy.

2 · · · Serve immediately, with white corn chips for dipping.

F
+
B
———

(BEER)

American pale ale is distinguished
from European and Australian ale by
the addition of assertive American
hops and a cleaner-flavoured yeast
in the brewing process. It has a clean,
crisp finish, which is what you want
with fresh flavours such as avocado
and tomato. It's quite fruity, too, and
a lovely choice to drink with spiced,
salty foods.

SALSA

I say the word 'salsa' and I think fresh and cheeky.
Like a dance of sorts: the flavours are for light fun
and a good time... and a pale lager!

6 **large ripe tomatoes**	
1 **small white onion** > *finely chopped*	
4 **garlic cloves** > *finely chopped*	
1 **jalapeño chilli** > *seeded and finely chopped*	
40 g *(1½ oz/1 cup)* **roughly chopped coriander** *(cilantro)*	
½ teaspoon **sea salt**	
1 tablespoon **lime juice**	
corn chips or tortilla chips > *to serve*	

SERVES 4

1 · · · **Use a small sharp knife to cut out the core of each tomato. Make a small cross-shaped incision in the opposite end, to make the tomatoes easier to peel.**

2 · · · **Put the tomatoes in a bowl and cover with boiling water. Leave for a few seconds, or until the skin starts to peel back from the flesh. Drain well. Peel the tomatoes and discard the skin.**

3 · · · **Cut the tomatoes in half and scoop out the seeds. Finely chop the tomatoes and toss together with the onion, garlic, chilli, coriander, salt and lime juice. Serve with corn chips or tortilla chips.**

JALAPEÑO POPPERS

You could use any large chilli, but plump jalapeños have large cavities particularly perfect for filling with cheese. The cream cheese here is combined with coriander and salt, but you could simply fill the jalapeño with a chunk of cheddar before crumbing and frying. We've been told how well matched wine is to cheese, but what about beer with cheese? Its carbonated fizz cleanses the fat from the palate and allows the flavour of the cheese to stand out. A wheat beer is a fine choice.

12 **jalapeño chillies**

125 g *(4½ oz)* **Ritz crackers**

250 g *(9 oz/1 cup)* **cream cheese** > *at room temperature*

2 tablespoons **finely chopped coriander** *(cilantro)*

½ teaspoon **sea salt**

2 **eggs**

150 g *(5½ oz/1 cup)* **plain** *(all-purpose)* **flour**

500 ml *(17 fl oz/2 cups)* **vegetable oil** > *for frying*

lime wedges > *to serve*

MAKES **12**

1 · · · Cut the chillies down the middle, without removing or cutting the stem. Use a small spoon to scrape out and discard the seeds. Put the crackers in a food processor and blitz until coarsely crumbed. Tip the crumbs onto a plate.

2 · · · Mix together the cream cheese, coriander and salt, then stuff into the chillies. Press the cut edges of the chillies together to enclose the filling.

3 · · · Beat the eggs in a bowl and put the flour in another bowl. Measure 250 ml (9 fl oz/1 cup) water into a third bowl.

4 · · · Dip the chillies in the water, then quickly roll in the flour to coat. Dip in the egg, then roll in the crumbs to coat. You can refrigerate these for up to a day before cooking.

5 · · · Heat the oil in a small saucepan over medium–high heat. Add some of the cracker crumbs to the oil. If they sizzle on contact, the oil is ready to cook in. Fry the chillies in batches for 2–3 minutes, turning them over in the oil so they are golden all over. Serve with lime wedges.

PORK AND CHORIZO EMPANADAS

These little pastry turnovers are typically served in Spain, Portugal and the many countries colonised by those two seafaring nations. Like many traditional recipes, the fillings vary depending on locally available ingredients and cultural influences. This is a traditional Spanish variety, but I have also eaten delicious kosher empanadas made with minced (ground) beef, chopped boiled egg and peas. These are just begging to be enjoyed with a dark ale or stout.

MAKES 12

2 tablespoons **olive oil**

1 **red onion** > *thinly sliced*

1 **chorizo sausage** > *diced*

500 g *(1 lb 2 oz)* **pork neck** > *cut into 5–6 cm (2–2½ inch) pieces*

2 teaspoons **Spanish smoked paprika**

2 teaspoons **ground cumin**

1 teaspoon **sea salt**

60 ml *(2 fl oz/¼ cup)* **red wine vinegar**

3 large sheets **frozen shortcrust pastry**

1 **egg** > *lightly beaten*

1 · · · **To make the filling, heat the oil in a saucepan over high heat and cook the onion for 4–5 minutes, or until softened. Add the chorizo and cook for 2–3 minutes, until the oil in the pan is coloured by the spices in the chorizo.**

2 · · · **Add the pork, paprika, cumin, salt and vinegar, stirring well to remove any bits stuck to the bottom of the pan.**

3 · · · **Add enough water to just cover the pork, then bring to the boil. Reduce the heat to a simmer and cook for about 1½ hours, or until the liquid has almost evaporated and the pork is very tender. Tip into a bowl and allow to cool, then mash to a chunky paste.**

4 · · · **Preheat the oven to 180°C (350°F). Cut twelve 10 cm (4 inch) circles from the pastry sheets. Put 1 heaped tablespoon of filling in the centre of each and use your fingers or a pastry brush to rub some water around the edge of the pastry. Bring the edges together and press to seal. Crimp or fold the pastry closed.**

5 · · · **Lay the pastries on a baking tray lined with baking paper. Brush with the egg and bake for 18–20 minutes, or until golden.**

TAPAS WINGS

I have run a tapas restaurant for several years with my great friend Jane. For some reason we overlooked putting these on the menu until another friend noticed we were missing this classic tapas snack. When we did start making them, they walked out the door. For the tasty result, this is surprisingly simple. Serve with a refreshing lager, such as a pilsener.

8 **chicken wings**

125 ml *(4 fl oz/½ cup)* **dry sherry**

2 teaspoons **Spanish smoked paprika**

½ teaspoon **sea salt**

1 tablespoon **lemon juice**

60 ml *(2 fl oz/¼ cup)* **olive oil**

6 **garlic cloves** > *coarsely crushed*

finely chopped flat-leaf *(Italian)* **parsley and lemon wedges** > *to serve*

M
A
K
E
S

8

1 ··· Cut the tips off the chicken wings and discard. Cut between the middle joint, to give 16 pieces of chicken. Place in a non-metallic bowl.

2 ··· Put the sherry in a small bowl and whisk in the paprika, salt, lemon juice, olive oil and garlic. Pour the mixture over the chicken and rub it all over the skin, using your hands. Cover and refrigerate for 6 hours, or overnight.

3 ··· Preheat the oven to 220°C (425°F). Tip the chicken pieces and marinade into a baking tray. Transfer to the oven and bake for 15 minutes.

4 ··· Turn the oven down to 180°C (350°F). Bake the wings for another 15 minutes, or until golden and cooked through. Serve with the parsley and lemon wedges.

F
+
B
—
(BEER)

Classic food deserves a classic beer. Salty, tangy, mildly spiced and just a bit greasy too, tapas works as a snack to keep the hunger wolves at bay. Tapas is quick to eat and calls for a chilled lager, quick to throw down, refreshing to the palate and with a hoppy froth. **Estrella** *(star)* lager from Barcelona is a gorgeous-tasting beer in a gorgeous bottle, with an international reputation.

MARTABAK

Indonesian dishes often take a back seat to Thai and Chinese in popularity, but I love the simple, earthy qualities of Indonesian cookery, where the flavours are rarely overdone. I would call this a spring roll, but it isn't a roll. The fragrant spices seem unusual, but they are also prevalent in Dutch cooking — the Dutch, of course, having once colonised Indonesia. A pale lager would be great with these.

16 x **20 cm** *(8 inch)* **square spring roll wrappers**

1 **egg** > *lightly beaten*

vegetable oil > *for frying*

1 **Lebanese** *(short)* **cucumber**

60 ml *(2 fl oz/¼ cup)* **white vinegar**

1 tablespoon **white sugar**

¼ teaspoon **sea salt**

kecap manis > *to serve*

MAKES
8

FILLING

1 tablespoon **vegetable oil**

1 **small leek** > *white part only* > *thinly sliced*

1 **large red chilli** > *thinly sliced*

500 g *(1 lb 2 oz)* **minced** *(ground)* **beef**

1 **garlic clove** > *finely chopped*

½ teaspoon **sea salt**

½ teaspoon **white pepper**

½ teaspoon **ground cinnamon**

large pinch **freshly grated nutmeg**

2 **cloves** > *finely ground*

4 **spring onions** *(scallions)* > *thinly sliced*

4 **eggs** > *beaten*

1 · · · To make the filling, heat the oil over high heat. Stir-fry the leek and chilli for 2–3 minutes, until the leek is silky soft. Add the beef, garlic and spices and stir-fry for 4–5 minutes, to brown the beef. Cool, then mix in the spring onion and egg.

2 · · · Lay the spring roll wrappers on a bench. Spread 3 tablespoons of the filling into a rectangle in the centre. Brush the pastry edges with beaten egg. Fold the end nearest you over the filling, fold in the sides, then roll up into a neat parcel.

3 · · · Heat 2 cm (¾ inch) vegetable oil in a frying pan over high heat. Cook the pastries in batches for 3–4 minutes, or until golden and crisp. Mix the remaining ingredients in a small bowl and serve with the hot parcels and kecap manis.

TEMPURA PRAWNS

Tempura is Japanese battered and fried food. The batter itself has taken on almost mythical status and much is written and passed down about its making. It couldn't be easier. Just remember two things: use icy-cold water and don't overbeat. Unlike custard, some little lumps are good in tempura batter. Tempura begs to be teamed with a Japanese rice lager, such as a super-dry Asahi.

S E R V E S

4

16 **large raw king prawns** *(shrimp)* > *peeled and deveined* > *tails intact*

vegetable oil > *for frying*

150 g *(5½ oz/1 cup)* **plain** *(all-purpose)* **flour**

pinch of **bicarbonate of soda** *(baking soda)*

1 **egg** > *beaten*

250 ml *(9 fl oz/1 cup)* **iced water**

shichimi togarashi *(Japanese seven-spice mix)* **and light soy sauce** > *to serve*

1 · · · Use a small knife to cut diagonal slashes across the belly of each prawn. Press gently down on the prawn to flatten: this will stop the prawns curling when fried.

2 · · · Half-fill a small saucepan with oil and heat over medium–high heat.

3 · · · Combine the flour and bicarbonate of soda in a bowl. Add the egg and iced water and use chopsticks or a fork to stir until most of the flour has been incorporated. A few lumps is fine — these give the fried batter a better texture.

4 · · · Holding the prawn by the tail, dip it in the batter to coat, then place into the hot oil. Use chopsticks to scatter some extra bits of batter onto the prawn and cook for 2–3 minutes, or until the batter is golden. Serve sprinkled with shichimi togarashi, with soy sauce for dipping.

FISH PAKORA

Put simply, 'pakora' means a food that is battered and fried, but it would be a shame to undersell this wonderful dish by labelling it in such shallow terms. This recipe is slightly more layered in flavour than the Green chilli pakora on page 19, and will easily stand up to a wheat beer.

400 g *(14 oz)* **fresh white fish fillets** > *such as pink ling*

¼ teaspoon **sea salt**

¼ teaspoon **freshly ground black pepper**

½ teaspoon **ground turmeric**

½ teaspoon **chilli powder**

vegetable oil > *for frying*

1 **large green chilli** > *thinly sliced*

mango chutney and lemon wedges > *to serve*

S E R V E S **4**

BATTER

75 g *(2½ oz/⅔ cup)* **besan** *(chickpea flour)*

½ teaspoon **hot paprika**

½ teaspoon **ground cumin**

1 tablespoon **lemon juice**

1 · · · Cut the fish into bite-sized pieces and sprinkle with the salt, pepper, turmeric and chilli powder. Toss the fish around to coat in the spices and set aside for 20–30 minutes.

2 · · · Combine the batter ingredients in a bowl. Whisk in enough water, about 125 ml (4 fl oz/½ cup), to give the mixture the consistency of thick custard. Toss the fish in the batter and set aside for 20–30 minutes.

3 · · · Half-fill a small frying pan with oil and heat over medium–high heat until shimmering. Fry the fish in batches for 3–4 minutes, or until the batter turns a golden caramel.

4 · · · Cook the green chilli slices in the oil for just a few seconds, then scatter over the fish. Serve with mango chutney and lemon wedges.

SEAFOOD SPRING ROLLS

These are small spring rolls, and most people could probably get through six to eight of them over a couple of Asian-style lagers. Anything rolled in pastry or rice paper is fussy, so I don't see the point in making a just a few of these rolls. Any uncooked rolls that are left over can be frozen.

MAKES **30**

30 x **20 cm** *(8 inch)* **round rice paper rolls**

vegetable oil > *for frying*

butter lettuce leaves and fresh mint > *to serve*

DIPPING SAUCE

60 ml *(2 fl oz/¼ cup)* **fish sauce**

60 ml *(2 fl oz/¼ cup)* **rice vinegar**

2 tablespoons **lime juice**

1 tablespoon **white sugar**

1 **small red chilli** > *finely chopped*

FILLING

4 **small dried shiitake mushrooms**

50 g *(1¾ oz)* **mung bean vermicelli noodles**

500 g *(1 lb 2 oz)* **minced** *(ground)* **pork**

100 g *(3½ oz)* **prawn** *(shrimp)* **meat** > *finely chopped*

125 g *(4½ oz/½ cup)* **crabmeat**

15 g *(½ oz/¼ cup)* **thinly sliced spring onions** *(scallions)*

40 g *(1½ oz/¼ cup)* **grated carrot**

2 **garlic cloves** > *finely chopped*

¼ teaspoon **freshly ground black pepper**

1 teaspoon **white sugar**

1 tablespoon **fish sauce**

2 tablespoons **cornflour** *(cornstarch)*

2 **eggs** > *beaten*

1 · · · To make the dipping sauce, combine all the ingredients in a bowl.

2 · · · To make the filling, put the mushrooms and noodles in a bowl and pour in enough boiling water to cover. Set aside for 10 minutes, or until the noodles are soft. Drain well.

3 · · · Finely chop the mushrooms and place in a large bowl. Snip the noodles into shorter lengths using kitchen scissors, to make them more manageable, then add to the mushrooms, along with the remaining filling ingredients. Use your hands to squeeze all the ingredients together so they are well combined.

4 · · · Lay a rice paper roll on a clean work surface. Brush the rice paper with cold water until it is no longer brittle, and has softened enough to fold. Put a tablespoon of the filling in the centre of the roll, roughly forming it into a small log shape.

5 · · · Fold the rice paper end nearest you over the filling, then fold in the sides of the roll. Roll up to enclose the filling to make a spring roll — but don't roll the paper up too firmly, or the spring rolls will burst when cooked.

6 · · · Half-fill a small saucepan with oil and heat over medium–high heat. When the surface of the oil is shimmering, cook the spring rolls in batches for 4–5 minutes, or until golden and crisp. Serve with the lettuce leaves, mint and the dipping sauce.

SEAFOOD SPRING ROLLS

CHILLI CHICKEN DRUMSTICKS

This dish is a holiday memory. The roadside cafes of Indonesia, known as warungs, each specialise in a street food unique to the region. So, a warung in Bali will serve different food to a warung in Java or Sumatra. This chicken recipe, ayam bumbu Bali, is fried chicken with a Balinese twist: lots of chilli, fragrant lime, and sweet and addictive kecap manis. A pale lager is the go here.

SERVES 4

10 **dried red chillies** > *about 5 cm (2 inches) long*

4 **garlic cloves**

1 tablespoon **palm sugar** *(jaggery)*

2 **tomatoes** > *chopped*

1 teaspoon **sea salt**

4 **lime leaves** > *roughly torn*

125 ml (*4 fl oz/½ cup*) **vegetable oil**

8 **large chicken drumsticks**

kecap manis > *to serve*

1 ··· Put the dried chillies in a heatproof bowl and cover with boiling water. Leave to soak for 30 minutes, then drain and cool. Pick the stem ends off the chillies. Rub the chillies between your thumb and fingers to loosen the seeds so they fall out. Remove as many seeds as possible.

2 ··· Chop the chillies and place in a food processor with the garlic, palm sugar, tomatoes and salt. Process to a sambal paste. Stir in the lime leaves.

3 ··· Preheat the oven to 180°C (350°F). Heat the oil in a frying pan over high heat. Fry the chicken drumsticks for 8 minutes, turning every 2 minutes, until golden all over.

4 ··· Lay the chicken pieces in a ceramic baking tray, so they fit snugly. Spread the chilli sambal over the chicken and bake for 30 minutes, or until cooked through. Serve hot, drizzled with kecap manis.

CHILLI SALT TOFU

I know die-hard meat-eaters who turn weak at the knees for this. When fried, this soft tofu becomes almost custard like, encased in a golden, crisp and spicy shell. Tofu is such a pure ingredient — don't mess with it too much, and certainly don't make burgers out of it or the meat-eaters will be running away at speed. A golden ale will be a fine friend indeed to this dish.

600 g *(1 lb 5 oz)* **soft tofu**

150 g *(5½ oz/1 cup)* **plain** *(all-purpose)* **flour**

500 ml *(17 fl oz/2 cups)* **vegetable oil** > *for frying*

2 **spring onions** *(scallions)* > *thinly sliced*

1 **large red chilli** > *thinly sliced*

lemon wedges > *to serve*

S E R V E S
4

CHILLI SALT

1 teaspoon **sea salt**

1 teaspoon **ground white pepper**

½ teaspoon **chilli powder**

1 · · · **To make the chilli salt, combine the ingredients in a small bowl.**

2 · · · **To prepare the tofu, carefully remove it from its packaging and drain on paper towel. The tofu may already be cut into 3–4 cm (1½ inch) cubes. If not, use a sharp knife to cut it into cubes, then pat dry with paper towel.**

3 · · · **Put the flour on a plate. Heat the oil in a saucepan or wok over medium-high heat. When the oil is shimmering, it is ready to use.**

4 · · · **Working in batches, gently roll the tofu in the flour. Use metal tongs to lower the tofu into the hot oil and cook, turning, for 2–3 minutes, or until crisp and golden. Drain on paper towel.**

5 · · · **When you've finished cooking all the tofu, add the spring onion and chilli to the hot oil and fry for 2–3 minutes, or until crisp. Scatter over the tofu. Serve sprinkled with the chilli salt, with lemon wedges on the side.**

FRIED CHEESE

This is a common snack in Eastern Europe, especially in the Czech Republic, the home of pilsener beer, or pils. Any cheesy fried thing is just destined to be tasty, but this is more shameful than most. Batter encases the cheese, making it twice as good (or bad, if you're a glass-half-empty sort of person). I would serve this with English pickle, cherry jam or even an Indian lime or mango pickle — and a pils, of course. Fried cheese and cold pilsener: there IS a god.

400 g *(14 oz)* **edam cheese**

75 g *(2½ oz/½ cup)* **plain** *(all-purpose)* **flour**

2 **eggs**

100 g *(3½ oz/1 cup)* **stale breadcrumbs**

light olive oil > *for frying*

sweet pickle, relish and lemon wedges > *to serve*

SERVES **4**

1 · · · Cut the cheese into slices no thicker than 1 cm (½ inch). Put the flour on a plate, beat the eggs in a bowl, and put the breadcrumbs in another bowl.

2 · · · Toss the cheese slices in the flour to coat. Dip in the egg, then dredge in the breadcrumbs to coat.

3 · · · Pour 1 cm (½ inch) oil into a frying pan and place over high heat. When the oil is shimmering, cook the cheese for 2 minutes on each side, or until golden. Serve hot with sweet pickle, relish and lemon wedges.

F+B

BEER

The word <u>pilsener</u> takes its name from the Czech city of Plzen, in which it was first brewed. Traditional Czech-style pilseners, made with Saaz hops, have a distinctive flavour: earthy and floral, herbal and spicy, with a sparkling golden finish. This clean, fresh-tasting lager sits nicely with salty, fried foods. Or you could head up the beer spectrum to a <u>wheat beer</u> or <u>golden ale</u>, especially if you accompany your fried snack with sweet condiments such as relishes, chutneys and mustard fruits.

HUMMUS

I put hummus and harissa next to each together here, although you'd be hard-pressed to find them on the same table geographically. Hummus hails from the western Middle East, and harissa is North African. But they really do get along very well together on any grilled meat sandwich, and with barbecued sausages or meatballs. And both of them go just fine with a good wheat beer.

220 g *(7¾ oz/1 cup)* **dried chickpeas**

2 **garlic cloves**

1 teaspoon **sea salt**

¼ teaspoon **ground white pepper**

1 tablespoon **lemon juice**

135 g *(4¾ oz/½ cup)* **tahini**

SERVES **4**

1 ··· Put the chickpeas in a bowl and cover with cold water. Soak overnight, then drain. Bring a saucepan of water to the boil. Add the chickpeas and cook for 45 minutes to 1 hour, or until very tender.

2 ··· Drain the chickpeas and, while still hot, quickly tip them into a food processor. Add the remaining ingredients and blend for 2–3 minutes, until you have a smooth, thick paste. Add 2–3 tablespoons cold water, to lighten the colour of the hummus and give it a lighter texture.

HARISSA

This recipe may seem to contain a huge quantity of chillies, and indeed it does
— but you do remove many of the seeds, and that's where the heat is. The harissa
simply gets better with age. If you refrigerate it for a couple of weeks, the flavour
becomes less dominated by the chilli heat and more complex and layered.

1 kg *(2 lb 4 oz)* **dried chillies** > *about 5 cm (2 inches) long*

3 **garlic cloves**

1 teaspoon **cumin seeds**

1 teaspoon **sea salt**

185 ml *(6 fl oz/¾ cup)* **olive oil**

SERVES **4**

1 ··· Soak the chillies in a bowl of hot water for about 1 hour. Drain well. Snap the stem ends off the chillies, then squeeze out as many of the hot seeds as you can.

2 ··· Roughly chop the chillies and place in a food processor with the garlic, cumin and salt. Blend until the chillies are finely chopped. Add the oil and process for a further 2–3 minutes, until you have a fine, well-combined paste.

3 ··· The harissa can be kept in a jar in the refrigerator for up to 3 weeks, by which time the oils will be fiery red.

2

LITTLE CRITTERS

How we love to eat these small critters, world over. By little critters, I mean mostly chickens, but we also have some recipes for duck and quail, and a very, very delicious way to cook rabbit. Chicken has to be the most eaten creature on the planet, right? A veritable edible international mascot, this bird is fried, curried, stewed and baked in every corner of the globe.

Roasty, toasty, malty, sweet beers are the go with these critters, especially when fragrant and aromatic spices are used — cinnamon, peppercorns and coriander seeds, to name a few. A lot of the recipes here include chilli (I just can't help myself). The gentle spices in the hops of lagers and ales are a fine match for the fiery heat of chilli.

AROMATIC WILD RABBIT WITH KRITHARAKI

Wild bunny scrubs up a treat in this classic Greek lamb recipe. If chicken is white meat, perhaps rabbit is a bottle blonde: white in parts; dark in others. Try this dish with a blonde, Belgian-style golden ale — a malty, hoppy, yeasty brew that is aromatic enough to flatter the oregano, without overpowering the dainty rabbit. The beer's hint of cheesiness also suits the pungent Greek sheep's milk cheese, kefalograviera. Kritharaki is a barley-shaped pasta traditionally served with lamb.

SERVES **4**

2–3 tablespoons **olive oil**

1 **wild rabbit** *(about 500 g/1 lb 2 oz)* > *cut into 10–12 pieces*

1 **onion** > *chopped*

3 **garlic cloves** > *chopped*

2 **cloves**

1 **cinnamon stick**

½ teaspoon **dried oregano**

2 **bay leaves**

1 **large ripe tomato** > *chopped*

1 tablespoon **tomato paste** *(concentrated purée)*

500 ml *(17 fl oz/2 cups)* **chicken stock**

125 ml *(4 fl oz/½ cup)* **red wine**

125 ml *(4 fl oz/½ cup)* **kritharaki** > *or orzo*

grated kefalograviera cheese and lemon cheeks > *to serve*

1 · · · **Preheat the oven to 220°C (425°F). Pour the oil into a casserole dish and heat in the oven for 10 minutes. Lay the rabbit pieces in a single layer in the dish and scatter with the onion, garlic, cloves, cinnamon, oregano and bay leaves. Season with sea salt and freshly ground black pepper.**

2 · · · **Return to the oven and bake for 20 minutes, or until the ingredients are aromatic, sizzling and turning golden. Turn the oven down to 180°C (350°F).**

3 · · · **Add the tomato, tomato paste, stock and red wine to the dish. Use a spoon or tongs to turn the rabbit pieces over, moving them around in the dish to mix well. Cover with foil, or put the lid on, then return to the oven and bake for a further 20 minutes.**

4 · · · **Add the kritharaki, stirring so the pasta settles in the pan. Cover and bake for another 20 minutes.**

5 · · · **Remove from the oven and leave covered for 10 minutes before serving. Serve sprinkled with kefalograviera, with lemon wedges on the side.**

BALINESE CHICKEN CURRY

Like most curries, except those containing seafood, this simple chicken curry will taste even better the next day. Serve with steamed white rice to soak up all that rich coconut sauce, and a crisp, refreshing beer, such as Bintang, to counterbalance the lovely, fragrant spices.

2 tablespoons **vegetable oil**

1 **whole chicken** > about 1.8 kg (4 lb) > *cut into 10–12 pieces*

4 x 300 ml *(10½ fl oz)* tins **coconut milk**

75 g *(2½ oz/½ cup)* **grated palm sugar** *(jaggery)*

60 ml *(2 fl oz/¼ cup)* **fish sauce** > *to taste*

6–8 **kaffir lime leaves**

500 ml *(17 fl oz/2 cups)* **chicken stock**

SERVES 4

CURRY PASTE

160 g *(5¾ oz/1 cup)* **peanuts**

8 **red Asian shallots** > *roughly chopped*

6 **garlic cloves**

5 cm *(2 inch)* chunk **fresh ginger** > *peeled and chopped*

6 **lemongrass stems** > *white part only* > *finely chopped*

1 tablespoon **coriander seeds**

1 tablespoon **black peppercorns**

4 **small red chillies** > *split lengthways*

1 teaspoon **ground turmeric**

1 · · · In a food processor, whiz the curry paste ingredients until finely chopped.

2 · · · Heat the oil in a large saucepan over medium–high heat. Cook the chicken in two batches, turning often, until golden all over. Remove the chicken, leaving the oil in the pan.

3 · · · Add the curry paste to the pan with 300 ml (10½ fl oz) of the coconut milk. Bring to the boil and stir to remove any bits stuck to the bottom of the pan. Cook for 8–10 minutes, or until the mixture is aromatic and golden yellow.

4 · · · Stir in the palm sugar and fish sauce and simmer for 2–3 minutes. Add the lime leaves, remaining coconut milk and stock and bring to the boil.

5 · · · Return the chicken to the pan. Bring to the boil, then simmer for about 45 minutes, or until the chicken is falling off the bone. Serve with steamed rice.

The great food of Indonesia's warungs, or streetside eateries, really appeals to me. So does the attitude: there *is* none. Coming from a country where licensing laws border on totalitarian, it's refreshingly relaxing to wander into a warung and be able to buy a plate of authentic Indonesian food and a cold <u>Bintang</u>, Indonesia's favourite beer. And I'm not sure I know of any other place whose local supermarkets have the same name as the local beer. The bintangs are great places to shop, as they carry most things under one roof, and are well-known landmarks for meeting up (handy if your sense of direction is as bad as mine). <u>Bintang</u> beer is clean, crisp and refreshing, with grassy, banana and lemon flavours. It is only lightly carbonated, so it does give the impression of going flat very quickly. Best drink it quick.

STIR-FRIED DUCK WITH PEPPER AND THAI BASIL

The green peppercorns used here aren't overly hot, but they do look good. They're usually sold in Asian food stores in glass jars, through which you can see all the little peppercorns attached to stems; if you can't get hold of them, use tinned French green peppercorns. In terms of heat, large red chillies can be hit or miss, so if spicy hot food is your thing, use a few chopped red bird's eye chillies instead and you'll be guaranteed a good time — especially with a golden ale in hand.

185 ml *(6 fl oz/¾ cup)* **vegetable oil**

2 **duck breast fillets** > *skin on*

2 tablespoons **fish sauce**

2 tablespoons **oyster sauce**

1 tablespoon **white sugar**

pinch of **ground white pepper**

2 **garlic cloves** > *finely chopped*

5 cm *(2 inch)* chunk **fresh ginger** > *peeled and finely chopped*

1 **large red chilli** > *thinly sliced on an angle*

1 **large red onion** > *sliced into thin wedges*

2 **strands green peppercorns in brine** > *drained*

large handful **Thai basil leaves**

steamed jasmine rice > *to serve*

SERVES **4**

1 · · · Heat the oil in a large non-stick frying pan over high heat. Place the duck, skin side down, in the pan and cook for 10 minutes, or until the skin is golden and crispy. Turn over and cook for another 10 minutes, or until the duck is just cooked through, but slightly pink in the centre. Transfer the duck to a plate, cover with foil and leave to rest for 10 minutes.

2 · · · Combine the fish sauce, oyster sauce, sugar and white pepper in a small bowl.

3 · · · Pour off all but 1 tablespoon of oil from the pan. Add the garlic and ginger and stir-fry for a few seconds, until softened. Now add the chilli, onion and peppercorns and stir-fry for 2–3 minutes, or until the onion has softened.

4 · · · Finely slice the duck, then add to the pan and stir-fry for 1 minute to combine with the other ingredients. Add the fish sauce mixture and stir to combine.

5 · · · Stir in half the Thai basil leaves. Scatter with the remaining basil leaves and serve with jasmine rice.

STIR-FRIED DUCK WITH PEPPER AND THAI BASIL

CRISP-SKINNED QUAIL WITH FIVE SPICE SALT

Quail are a very popular menu item in Vietnam, possibly due to the French influence, although the flavours here are essentially Chinese. True, quail are bony and fiddly, but they're also very sweet in flavour, and in looks. They also crisp up a real treat when deep-fried — and because they are small, they are an easy bird to deep-fry at home without too much fuss and bother. Sip a lager with these spicy, tasty morsels.

60 ml *(2 fl oz/¼ cup)* **light soy sauce**

60 ml *(2 fl oz/¼ cup)* **dark soy sauce**

2 **star anise**

1 **cinnamon stick**

1 tablespoon **sea salt**

1 tablespoon **white sugar**

4 **large quail**

vegetable oil > *for frying*

iceberg lettuce wedges and lemon wedges > *to serve*

SERVES 4

SPICED SALT

½ teaspoon **Chinese five spice**

½ teaspoon **ground white pepper**

1 tablespoon **sea salt**

1 · · · Combine the spiced salt ingredients in a small airtight container.

2 · · · In a large saucepan, bring the soy sauces, spices, salt, sugar and 3 litres (102 fl oz/12 cups) water to the boil. Cook for 5 minutes. Add the quail, fully immersing them. Take the pan off the heat, cover tightly and leave for 1 hour.

3 · · · Transfer the quail to a large plate, draining off any excess liquid. Refrigerate until completely chilled, preferably overnight.

4 · · · Leave the quail at room temperature for 1 hour. To cut the quail, sit a quail on a chopping board, breast side up. Insert a small, sharp knife into the quail and cut down each side of the backbone. Discard the backbone. Cut each quail in half between the breasts. Cut between the drumstick and the breast, to give two drumsticks. Cut between the wing and the body, to give two wings. Now cut each breast crossways in half, to give eight pieces from each quail.

5 · · · Half-fill a large saucepan with oil. Heat the oil over high heat until shimmering. Fry the quail in two batches, for 2–3 minutes, or until just cooked through, turning them around in the oil until golden and crisp. Drain on paper towel. Serve with lettuce, lemon wedges and the spiced salt.

THAI BARBECUED CHICKEN SALAD

Typical of much of Thai food, there is a rollercoaster of flavours here. And, again typical of Thai food, it's all about the balance: the sweetness of the sugar, the saltiness of the fish sauce, and the tang or sourness of the lime and tamarind. But the best thing of all is that you don't have to go too far out of your way to make this knockout, authentic Thai salad, before relaxing with a wheat beer.

½ **barbecued chicken**

3 **large dried red chillies**

1 **large red onion** > *very thinly sliced*

large handful **mint leaves**

40 g *(1½ oz/1 cup)* **chopped coriander** *(cilantro)*

2 tablespoons **coconut cream**

steamed jasmine rice and lime wedges > *to serve*

SERVES 4

DRESSING

1 tablespoon **chilli jam**

2 teaspoons **brown sugar**

1 tablespoon **tamarind purée**

1 tablespoon **fish sauce**

1 tablespoon **lime juice**

¼ teaspoon **ground white pepper**

1 ··· Combine the dressing ingredients in a small bowl and set aside.

2 ··· Remove the skin from the chicken. Finely slice the skin and place in a large bowl. Roughly shred the meat and add to the bowl.

3 ··· Put the dried chillies in a frying pan and cook over high heat, shaking the pan, until the chillies start to smoke and blister. Tip them onto a chopping board. When they are cool enough to handle, roughly chop and add to the chicken with the onion, mint and coriander. Use your hands to gently toss together.

4 ··· Pour the dressing over the salad and gently toss to coat. Tumble into a large serving bowl or onto a plate. Spoon the coconut cream over and serve with jasmine rice, with lime wedges on the side.

TURMERIC AND LEMONGRASS GRILLED CHICKEN

Here the chicken is cooked in a wok or frying pan, but feel free to fire up the barbecue for this one. The only real trick with this simple recipe is to know that the spice paste on the chicken is pretty dry, so you need to watch carefully to make sure it doesn't burn. The raw ingredients in the spice paste need some cooking, so be patient, take your time, then reward yourself with a palate-pleasing pilsener.

6 **skinless chicken thigh fillets**

60 ml *(2 fl oz/¼ cup)* **vegetable oil**

coriander *(cilantro)* **sprigs, lime wedges and steamed jasmine rice** > *to serve*

SERVES 4

LEMONGRASS SPICE PASTE

6 **garlic cloves** > *chopped*

2 **red Asian shallots** > *sliced*

1 **lemongrass stem** > *white part chopped*

2 tablespoons **mild curry powder**

½ teaspoon **ground white pepper**

1 teaspoon **ground turmeric**

2 tablespoons **light soy sauce**

1 · · · You can trim the fat off the chicken thighs, if need be — although I prefer to leave the fat on them as it gives a juicier result when cooking with intense heat, as we will be here. Place the chicken in a bowl.

2 · · · Put the spice paste ingredients in a food processor and blitz to a coarse paste. Use your hands to rub the spice paste all over the chicken thighs. Cover and refrigerate for 3–6 hours, or even overnight.

3 · · · Heat a large wok or frying pan over high heat. Add the oil and swirl to coat well. Lay the chicken pieces in the hot pan and scrape any paste left in the bowl over the chicken. Turn the heat down a little towards medium. Cook the chicken for 7–8 minutes, then turn and cook for a further 5–6 minutes — the chicken should have a rough, curry-coloured crust. Remove from the wok and allow to cool a little.

4 · · · Slice the chicken into strips about 2 cm (¾ inch) thick. Scatter with coriander and serve with lime wedges and steamed jasmine rice.

F + B

BEER

The first choice of beer to enjoy with chicken cooked in Thai spices would be a crisp, clean Thai ale. <u>Singha</u>, <u>Chang</u> or <u>Lao</u> are the top three, in order of quality. <u>Chang</u> is a popular choice for young players, with a relatively high alcohol volume content giving it the nickname 'chang-over'.

NORTHERN CHINESE CHICKEN SALAD

This is fresh, fast and tasty, but at first glance an odd salad. Did I say salad? Generally, salady dishes do not go with beer because their ingredients, such as tomatoes and vinegar, tend to be acidic. I was introduced to this tasty flavour combination in a number of Northern Chinese restaurants that have popped up in Sydney. Lager is a lovely choice with this one.

SERVES 4

1 **roast chicken or Chinese soy chicken** *(see note)*

6 **spring onions** *(scallions)* > *thinly sliced*

2 **Lebanese** *(short)* **cucumbers** > *halved, seeded and thinly sliced*

2 teaspoons **sichuan peppercorns**

2 teaspoons **sea salt**

10 g *(¼ oz/¼ cup)* **coriander** *(cilantro)* **leaves**

DRESSING

1 teaspoon **white sugar**

2 tablespoons **light soy sauce**

2 teaspoons **sesame oil**

2 teaspoons **chilli oil**

1 · · · Remove the skin from the chicken and discard. Pick all the meat off the chicken frame and pull it apart into thin strands. Place in a large bowl, along with the spring onion and cucumber.

2 · · · Put the peppercorns in a dry frying pan over high heat. Shake the pan until the peppercorns start to smoke and crackle. Remove from the heat and allow to cool. Put the peppercorns and salt in a spice mill or use a mortar and pestle to grind to a rough-looking powder.

3 · · · Mix together the dressing ingredients and pour over the chicken. Toss gently to coat. Sprinkle with the peppercorns and salt, to taste. Scatter with the coriander and serve.

NOTE: *Chinese soy chickens can be bought from Chinese barbecue restaurants in Chinatown areas in larger cities. The glossy chicken is dunked in a soy sauce mixture, and the meat is very tender and full of flavour.*

GENERAL TSO'S CHICKEN

I would not say this is a traditional Chinese dish — it's more in the spirit of the chicken tikka masala served in Indian restaurants in Britain, and the Mongolian lamb of Australia's Chinese restaurants. You'd be hard-pressed to find a similar, authentic item in a restaurant in China, yet General Tso's chicken is a staple in American Chinese restaurants. When done well, its balance of flavours is universally appreciated. Try it with a golden ale.

SERVES **4**

2 tablespoons **Chinese rice wine**

1 tablespoon **light soy sauce**

1 **egg**

4 **free-range skinless chicken thigh fillets** > *cut into large chunks*

vegetable oil > *for frying*

75 g *(2½ oz/½ cup)* **plain** *(all-purpose)* **flour**

2 **garlic cloves** > *chopped*

5 cm *(2 inch)* chunk **fresh ginger** > *peeled and thinly sliced*

3 **spring onions** *(scallions)* > *cut into short lengths*

steamed jasmine rice > *to serve*

SAUCE

60 ml *(2 fl oz/¼ cup)* **chicken stock**

1 tablespoon **light soy sauce**

1 tablespoon **rice vinegar**

1 tablespoon **hoisin sauce**

1 tablespoon **sesame oil**

1 tablespoon **chilli bean paste**

1 tablespoon **white sugar**

1 teaspoon **cornflour** *(cornstarch)*

1 · · · Whisk the rice wine, soy sauce and egg in a bowl with a pinch each of ground white pepper, sea salt and sugar. Add the chicken, stirring to coat in the marinade. Cover and set aside for 30 minutes, or refrigerate for 3–6 hours.

2 · · · Fill a wok one-third full of oil. Heat over high heat until the oil is shimmering. Stir the flour through the chicken to make a thick batter. In two batches, fry the chicken in the hot oil for about 3–4 minutes, or until golden.

3 · · · Drain all but 1 tablespoon of oil from the wok. Add the garlic, ginger and spring onion and stir-fry for 1–2 minutes. Combine the sauce ingredients, add to the wok and bring to the boil, then keep boiling until the sauce thickens.

4 · · · Stir the chicken through the sauce until coated. Serve with jasmine rice.

CHICKEN TIKKA MASALA

Some say this is the most ordered restaurant menu item in the United Kingdom and has taken over from fish and chips as the nation's favourite food. True, this make-at-home version has a lengthy list of ingredients, but please don't let that deter you. The marinated chicken could be a meal in its own right; just cook for a little longer than specified here and serve with a simple salad of tomato and onion (kachumbari)... and a pilsener!

6 **skinless chicken thigh fillets** > *each cut into three pieces*

2 tablespoons **vegetable oil**

65 g *(2¼ oz/¼ cup)* **plain yoghurt**

60 ml *(2 fl oz/¼ cup)* **thin** *(pouring)* **cream**

1 teaspoon **garam masala**

steamed basmati rice, coriander *(cilantro)* **and lemon wedges** > *to serve*

CHICKEN MARINADE

60 ml *(2 fl oz/¼ cup)* **lemon juice**

2 teaspoons **sea salt**

125 g *(4½ oz/½ cup)* **plain yoghurt**

1 tablespoon **finely grated fresh ginger**

1 tablespoon **crushed garlic**

1 tablespoon **ground cumin**

1 tablespoon **ground coriander**

2 teaspoons **garam masala**

1 teaspoon **ground turmeric**

1 teaspoon **chilli powder**

¼ teaspoon **freshly ground black pepper**

SAUCE

2 **onions** > *chopped*

1 tablespoon **chopped fresh ginger**

6 **garlic cloves** > *chopped*

2 tablespoons **ghee or butter**

4 **cardamom pods**

1 **cinnamon stick**

1 teaspoon **sweet paprika**

400 g *(14 oz)* tin **chopped tomatoes**

1 tablespoon **tomato paste** *(concentrated purée)*

1 teaspoon **sea salt**

1 teaspoon **white sugar**

1 · · · Place the chicken on a chopping board and use a sharp knife to cut several diagonal slashes across each piece. Put the chicken in a non-metallic bowl with the lemon juice and 1 teaspoon of the salt, rubbing the mixture into the slashes. Set aside for about 30 minutes.

2 · · · Put the remaining marinade ingredients, including the remaining 1 teaspoon salt, in a non-metallic bowl and whisk until well combined. Tip the chicken and any juices into the marinade and use your hands to rub the marinade into the chicken. Cover and refrigerate overnight.

3 · · · To make the sauce, put the onion, ginger and garlic in a food processor and blend to a paste. Heat the ghee in a saucepan over medium–high heat. When the ghee has melted and is sizzling, add the onion paste and stir-fry for 1 minute to combine. Cook for a further 2–3 minutes, stirring every now and then, until the paste no longer has that raw onion aroma.

4 · · · Stir in the cardamom, cinnamon and paprika and cook for 1–2 minutes. Stir in the tomatoes, tomato paste, salt and sugar and cook for 4–5 minutes, so the sauce is just simmering. Allow to cool, then transfer to a food processor and whiz to a smooth sauce. Pour the sauce into a saucepan. Keep warm over low heat while cooking the chicken.

5 · · · Heat the oil in a frying pan over high heat. Cook the chicken for 5 minutes on each side, or until golden. Put the chicken pieces into the sauce and cook over low heat for 10 minutes, or until the chicken is cooked all the way through.

6 · · · Gently stir in the yoghurt, cream and garam masala. Serve with basmati rice, coriander and lemon wedges.

CHICKEN TIKKA MASALA

How about serving Indian spiced curries with <u>saison</u>, a traditional French farmhouse beer? There you have it: the crazy world of food and beer. In a broad sense, <u>saison</u> is a pale ale. It is fruity, spicy and summery, with hints of citrus, and has an unmistakable flavour and rich notes. It's no surprise that this traditional favourite of peasant field-workers is now loved by modern-day beer drinkers around the world.

ROAST DUCK WITH VEAL AND APPLE STUFFING

The Europeans and Chinese do roast duck so well. That's a generalisation, to be sure, but one few would disagree with. Roast duck can be paired beautifully with a stuffing with fruits, as well as meat such as pork and veal. I was once afraid of cooking duck, until I realised all you have to do is cook it like chicken, only for a little longer, until the skin makes you want to rip it off and eat it. So, that just about covers the cooking instructions. And for drinking? A stout or dark ale.

SERVES 4

1.8 kg *(4 lb)* **duck** > *washed and patted dry*

100 g *(3½ oz)* **minced** *(ground)* **veal**

100 g *(3½ oz)* **minced** *(ground)* **pork**

1 **egg** > *beaten*

40 g *(1½ oz/½ cup)* **fresh breadcrumbs**

2 **green apples** > *peeled and cored* > *grated*

1 teaspoon **marjoram leaves**

BRAISED CABBAGE AND APPLE

½ **red cabbage** > *outer leaves and core removed* > *finely shredded*

60 ml *(2 fl oz/¼ cup)* **red wine vinegar**

1 teaspoon **sea salt**

2 tablespoons **sugar**

2 **bacon rashers** > *rind removed* > *chopped*

2 **green apples** > *peeled and cored* > *cut into thin strips*

1 **onion** > *finely chopped*

1 ... Preheat the oven to 220°C (425°F). Use a sharp knife to cut off and discard the neck from the duck, and any extra fat around the cavity. In a bowl, mix the veal, pork, egg, breadcrumbs, apple and marjoram with your hands until well combined. Push the stuffing into the duck and seal the cavity with toothpicks.

2 ... Place the duck in a roasting tray and bake for 20 minutes, or until the skin is starting to turn golden and the fat is rendering. Turn the oven down to 160°C (315°F). Roast the duck for a further 2 hours, basting it with the rendered fat. Remove from the oven, cover with foil and rest for 30 minutes before carving.

3 ... Meanwhile, toss the cabbage with the vinegar, salt and sugar; set aside. Heat a heavy-based saucepan over high heat. Fry the bacon for 2–3 minutes, or until golden and releasing some of its fat. Add the apple and onion. Stir for about 1 minute, then reduce the heat to medium, cover and cook for 5–6 minutes. Add the cabbage and 185 ml (6 fl oz/¾ cup) boiling water. Stir to remove bits stuck to the pan. Cover and cook over low heat for 1½ hours, stirring occasionally, until the cabbage is very tender and aromatic. Serve hot or warm, with the duck.

CHICKEN WITH CAPSICUM, OLIVES AND HAM

This may look like a recipe from a contemporary food magazine, but it's actually an old Spanish dish, pollo al chilindrón — a simple, rich stew that is just delicious, trendy or not. A well-hopped dark ale isn't an obvious choice here, but pairs well with the extra depth from the ham, olives and paprika. The flavours of this dish will 'warm up' as it cools down, meaning it tastes better if not eaten piping hot. Conversely, the flavours in the dark ale will benefit from not being too cold.

SERVES **4**

4 **ripe tomatoes**

8 **skinless chicken thigh fillets**

60 ml *(2 fl oz/¼ cup)* **olive oil**

2 **onions** > *sliced into thin wedges*

6 **garlic cloves** > *chopped*

100 g *(3½ oz)* **sliced ham**

1 **green capsicum** *(pepper)* > *roughly chopped*

1 **red capsicum** *(pepper)* > *roughly chopped*

2 teaspoons **smoked paprika**

90 g *(3¼ oz/½ cup)* **green olives**

90 g *(3¼ oz/½ cup)* **black Spanish olives**

small handful **flat-leaf** *(Italian)* **parsley sprigs**

crusty bread > *to serve*

1··· Use a small, sharp knife to cut the core out of each tomato, and cut a small cross in the opposite end. Put the tomatoes in a bowl and cover with boiling water. Leave for just a minute, then drain and rinse under cold water. Peel the tomatoes and cut in half. Scoop the seeds out and finely chop the flesh.

2··· Season the chicken with sea salt and freshly ground black pepper. Heat the oil in a heavy-based saucepan or frying pan over medium–high heat. Cook the chicken for 2–3 minutes on each side, or until golden brown. Remove to a plate.

3··· Add the onion, garlic, ham and capsicums to the pan, stirring well to separate the onion wedges. Reduce the heat to medium, then cover and cook for 10 minutes, stirring every couple of minutes. Add the tomato, then cover and cook for another 5 minutes.

4··· Return the chicken to the pan and stir to coat. Stir in the paprika. Cover and cook for a further 10 minutes, or until the chicken is cooked through.

5··· Stir in the olives and parsley. Cook for a couple of minutes to heat the olives through. Serve warm, with crusty bread.

FRIED CHICKEN

There's some magic at play here. The marinade is thick and creamy from the inclusion of buttermilk, so make sure you let the chicken marinate for a good while, as the buttermilk apparently does something nice to the chicken during this time. Tossing the chicken around in the flour will initially coat it in a gloopy mass that will almost miraculously turn into a golden, crispy crust when fried. Serving it with a lager just adds to the magic.

500 ml *(17 fl oz/2 cups)* **buttermilk**

1 tablespoon **Tabasco sauce**

1 teaspoon **cayenne pepper**

2 teaspoons **garlic powder**

2 teaspoons **sweet paprika**

4 **chicken drumsticks** > *skin on*

4 **chicken thighs** > *bone in and skin on*

450 g *(1 lb/3 cups)* **plain** *(all-purpose)* **flour**

3 teaspoons **ground white pepper**

1 teaspoon **sea salt**

vegetable oil > *for frying*

SERVES **4**

1 · · ·   In a non-metallic bowl, combine the buttermilk, Tabasco, ½ teaspoon of the cayenne pepper, and 1 teaspoon each of the garlic powder and paprika.

2 · · ·   Add the chicken pieces and use your hands or tongs to evenly coat. Cover and refrigerate for 6 hours, or preferably overnight. Remove the chicken from the refrigerator 30 minutes before cooking.

3 · · ·   Preheat the oven to 160°C (315°F). Put the flour, white pepper, salt and remaining cayenne pepper, garlic powder and paprika in a clean plastic or brown paper bag. Add the chicken and toss around in the bag to thickly coat.

4 · · ·   Pour enough oil into a large frying pan or heavy-based flameproof casserole dish so that the chicken will be fully covered by oil during cooking. Heat the oil over medium–high heat until shimmering.

5 · · ·   Add half the chicken, skin-side up, and fry for 2 minutes; the oil will sizzle and froth, ensuring the skin is crisp and golden. Reduce the heat to low and fry for a further 15 minutes, using tongs to turn the chicken pieces, and making sure the skin doesn't stick to the bottom of the pan.

6 · · ·   Remove the chicken to a plate, cover with foil and place in the oven to keep warm. Reheat the oil over high heat and cook the remaining chicken in the same way. Great served with mashed potato and steamed beans.

CHICKEN IN GARLIC AND VINEGAR

This is a variation of adobo, a dish with dominant flavours of soy, garlic and vinegar that's indigenous to the Philippines. We also find the same fab combination of garlic and vinegar in the vindaloo curry of India, where the Portuguese penchant for those flavourings fused with the local cuisine. You can't go past a pilsener with this one.

SERVES **4**

4 **skinless chicken leg quarters**

2 tablespoons **vegetable oil**

1 **onion** > *halved and cut into thin wedges*

¼ teaspoon **cayenne pepper**

6 **garlic cloves** > *roughly chopped*

2 **bay leaves**

4 **red chillies** > *halved*

170 ml *(5½ fl oz/⅔ cup)* **sherry vinegar**

80 ml *(2½ fl oz/⅓ cup)* **soy sauce**

1 teaspoon **whole black peppercorns**

1 teaspoon **chilli flakes**

3 tablespoons **flat-leaf parsley** > *finely chopped*

1 . . . Cut each piece of chicken between the thigh and the drumstick to give eight pieces. Heat 1 tablespoon of the oil in a heavy-based saucepan over high heat. Cook the chicken in two batches, for 8–10 minutes, turning every couple of minutes until golden. Remove from the pan.

2 . . . Add the remaining oil to the pan and cook the onion for 4–5 minutes, or until it has softened, stirring to break up the wedges. Add the cayenne pepper, garlic, bay leaves and chilli halves and stir-fry for 1 minute, or until fragrant.

3 . . . Add the vinegar and bring to the boil, stirring to remove any bits stuck to the bottom of the pan. Stir in the soy sauce, peppercorns and chilli flakes. Return the chicken to the pan. Bring to the boil, reduce the heat and simmer for 30 minutes, or until the chicken is just cooked through.

4 . . . Just before serving, stir the parsley through. Fried potatoes or green beans would make a great accompaniment.

KARAAGE

Karaage is Japanese fried chicken. Along with such faves as tonkatsu (crumbed fried pork) and tempura (battered and fried anything), karaage is testament to the diversity of Japanese cooking. It's not all about raw fish and omega-3s. Japanese cooking can also be fabulous comfort food, especially with a fine Japanese lager to help wash it all down.

750 g *(1 lb 10 oz)* **boneless chicken thigh fillets, skin on** > *cut into 3 cm (1¼ inch) pieces*

150 g *(5½ oz/1 cup)* **potato flour**

vegetable oil > *for frying*

shredded iceberg lettuce, steamed white rice and lemon wedges > *to serve*

SERVES
4

MARINADE

5 cm *(2 inch)* chunk **fresh ginger** > *peeled*

125 ml *(4 fl oz/½ cup)* **Japanese soy sauce**

80 ml *(2½ fl oz/⅓ cup)* **mirin**

2 tablespoons **Japanese rice vinegar**

1 · · · **To make the marinade, finely grate the ginger onto a clean, thin piece of cloth. Use the cloth to squeeze the juice from the ginger into a bowl large enough to marinate the chicken in. Add the soy sauce, mirin and vinegar and stir well.**

2 · · · **Add the chicken to the marinade, stirring to coat. Cover and refrigerate for a couple of hours.**

3 · · · **Remove the chicken from the refrigerator 30 minutes before cooking. Put the potato flour in a bowl.**

4 · · · **Pour enough oil in a saucepan to come halfway up the side of the pan. Heat over medium–high heat until shimmering.**

5 · · · **Using chopsticks or tongs, remove several chicken pieces from the marinade, shaking off any excess. Toss the chicken in the flour, then cook in the hot oil for 4–5 minutes, or until golden. Drain the cooked chicken on paper towel.**

6 · · · **Give the oil a little time to reheat, then cook the remaining chicken, reducing the heat if needed (you don't want the chicken to burn before it's cooked through). Serve with lettuce, rice and lemon wedges.**

F+B

BEER

The four big lager breweries in Japan are <u>Asahi</u>, <u>Kirin</u>, <u>Sapporo</u> and <u>Suntory</u>. The Japanese pride in the quality, provenance and craftsmanship of their food also extends to beer brewing, which is of a similarly high standard. A palate-cleansing pale ale is my beer of choice with most fried foods.

DEVIL'S CHICKEN

To 'devil' food means to cook it with spice or chilli heat, although the spice heat in English dishes such as devilled kidneys or eggs has nothing on Asian devilled recipes, where it isn't unusual to see cupfuls of dried chillies added. Don't be put off by all the dried chillies here; it all balances out in the end. Still, a little fear and trepidation are what you want with hot food. You want to look at a chilli jam, harissa or sambal and be a little afraid. A wheat beer goes wickedly well with this.

SERVES **4**

1 **whole chicken** > *about 1.6 kg (3 lb 8 oz)*
60 ml *(2 fl oz/¼ cup)* **vegetable oil**
2 **large onions** > *quartered*
6 **garlic cloves** > *chopped*
5 cm *(2 inch)* chunk **fresh ginger** > *peeled and cut into thin matchsticks*
2 **large red chillies**
1 teaspoon **sea salt**
2 tablespoons **sugar**
1 tablespoon **soy sauce**
125 ml *(4 fl oz/½ cup)* **white vinegar**
6–8 **small waxy potatoes** > *peeled*
steamed basmati or long-grain white rice > *to serve*

SPICE PASTE

30 **dried chillies** > *about 5 cm (2 inches) long*
8 **red Asian shallots** > *chopped*
3 cm *(1¼ inch)* chunk **fresh turmeric** > *peeled and chopped*
3 cm *(1¼ inch)* chunk **fresh galangal** > *peeled and chopped*
2 **lemongrass stems** > *white part only* > *sliced*
1 teaspoon **brown mustard seeds**
1 tablespoon **vegetable oil**

1 · · · To make the spice paste, snap the hard stem end off the dried chillies, then shake out and discard the seeds. This will remove the heat, but leave that lovely chilli flavour. Soak the chillies in a bowl of boiling water for about 30 minutes.

2 · · · Roughly chop the chillies, placing them in a food processor. Add the remaining spice paste ingredients and blend for 2–3 minutes, adding 2–3 tablespoons water to make a thick, chunky paste. Transfer to a bowl and refrigerate until needed.

3 · · · Use a large knife or cleaver to chop the chicken. To do this, remove each leg and thigh from the body, then cut between the leg and thigh joint to give four pieces in total. Remove the wings, then cut off and discard the wing tips. (I generally remove the entire part of the chicken under the breasts and reserve it for making stock.) This will leave both breasts intact to the breastbone. Cut lengthways between the breastbone cartilage. Cut each breast crossways into three pieces to give six pieces. You will now have 12 pieces of chicken, so put them all in a bowl and refrigerate until needed.

4 · · · Heat the oil in a heavy-based saucepan over high heat. Cook the onion, garlic, ginger, chillies and salt for 2–3 minutes, stirring the onion around so the individual segments separate and soften.

5 · · · Add the spice paste and stir to combine. Reduce the heat to medium and cook for 5–6 minutes, or until fragrant, making sure you don't burn the paste. Add the chicken and stir to coat all over in the spices.

6 · · · Increase the heat to high. Stir in the sugar, soy sauce, vinegar and 1 litre (35 fl oz/4 cups) water, then bring the sauce to the boil. Add the potatoes, reduce the heat and simmer, uncovered, for 45 minutes, by which time the chicken and potatoes will be cooked through and the sauce will take on a fiery colour. Serve with rice.

DEVIL'S CHICKEN

PIRI PIRI CHICKEN MOZAMBIQUE

We just can't seem to get enough of fast-food chicken. There has been a huge rise in outlets selling what is loosely termed 'Portuguese chicken', the defining element being the inclusion of piri piri sauce as a seasoning or marinade. Piri piri, however, is not confined to Portugal, or indeed fast-food chicken outlets — this fiery, addictive concoction is also prevalant throughout Mozambique, Angola, Namibia and South Africa. Pilsener and piri piri: another popular pairing.

2 **small whole chickens**

light olive oil > *for frying*

SERVES 4

PIRI PIRI SAUCE

100 g *(3½ oz)* **small red chillies** > *seeded and roughly chopped*

6 **garlic cloves** > *chopped*

1 **large onion** > *chopped*

250 ml *(9 fl oz/1 cup)* **white vinegar**

1 teaspoon **sea salt**

1 teaspoon **white sugar**

1 teaspoon **ground white pepper**

½ teaspoon **freshly ground black pepper**

2 tablespoons **lime juice**

1 · · · **To make the piri piri sauce, blend the chilli, garlic, onion and half the vinegar in a food processor; it doesn't need to be too smooth. Pour the sauce into a small saucepan. Add the remaining ingredients and bring to the boil. Cover and cook over low heat for 45 minutes, or until thickened. Set aside to cool.**

2 · · · **Sit the chickens on a chopping board, breast side down, legs and cavity facing you. Using kitchen scissors, cut down one side of the parson's nose (tail), cutting through the little rib bones attached to the backbone. Now cut the other side of the backbone and reserve it for making stock. Turn the birds over. Firmly press with the palm of your hand on the breastbone to flatten. Make several, deep diagonal slashes across each bird, cutting through the meat to the bone.**

3 · · · **Rub 2–3 tablespoons piri piri sauce over the skin side of each chicken, and into the cuts (save any remaining sauce for serving). Marinate in the fridge for 3–6 hours, or even overnight. Remove the chicken from the fridge 1 hour before cooking.**

4 · · · **Preheat the oven to 220°C (425°F). Heat a frying pan over high heat. Add some oil and cook a batch of chicken, skin side down, for 3–4 minutes, or until golden. Transfer to a baking tray and repeat with the remaining chicken. Bake for 20–25 minutes, or until cooked through; the juices should run clear when skewered between the drumstick and the breast. Serve with any remaining piri piri sauce.**

3

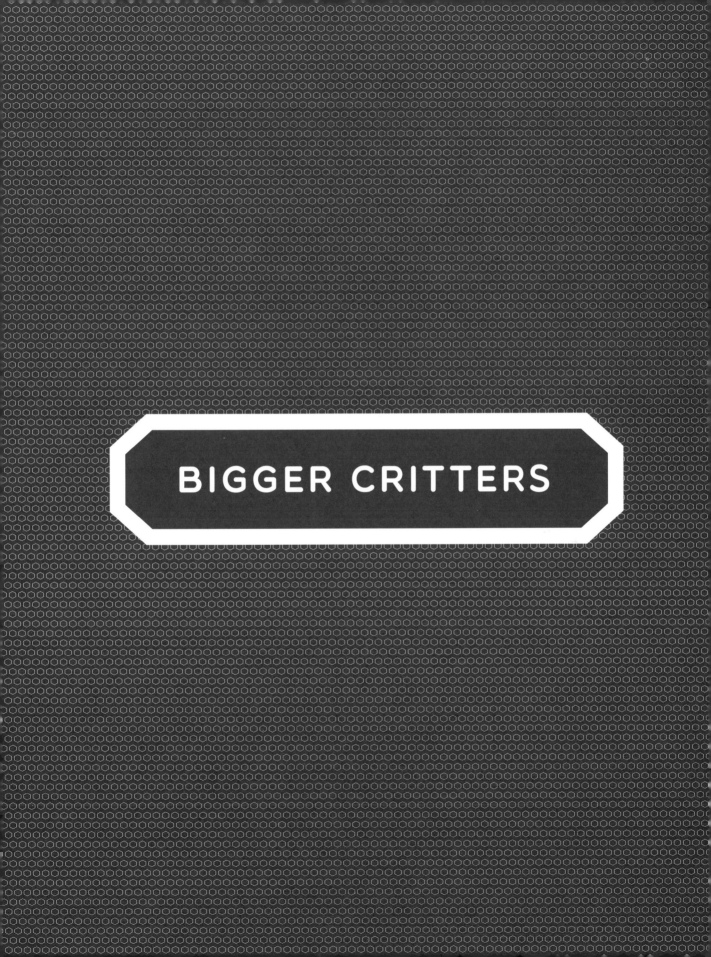

BIGGER CRITTERS

We're talking larger mammals here: beef, pork and lamb. Is it just me, or is it more enjoyable to eat when the weather's cold? Slow-cooked fare is what I want when the temperature drops: warming, complex, long-cooked flavours. And heartier food, of course, deserves a heartier brew.

Some of the recipes in this chapter use beer in the cooking, so pairing the food with the brew is easy... and, if you have any beer left over from the recipe, you'll know what to do with that!

Nothing too cold should be drunk with these dishes. Buttery, unctuous fare deserves grainy, caramel, sweet or dry beer. Big, robust food needs big, bold beer. Even a pulled-pork taco, with its rich, complex flavours, loves stout or dark ale. So if creamy, full-bodied brews are your thing, dog-ear these pages.

SLOW-COOKED LAMB SHOULDER WITH STOUT

It is not uncommon to see lamb paired with honey, especially in the Middle East and North Africa. In many Moroccan recipes, cooked lamb is drizzled with honey or added to tagines. The sweet, dark honey flavours in stout are perfect with lamb, and the combination makes for a great slow-cooked recipe. Don't eat this straight from the oven — leave it for an hour or so and drink with a slightly chilled stout.

SERVES 4

2 tablespoons **olive oil**

1 **lamb shoulder** > *about 2 kg (4 lb 8 oz)*

2 **onions** > *halved and sliced into wedges*

4 **garlic cloves** > *roughly chopped*

1 **large rosemary sprig**

1 **bay leaf**

250 ml *(9 fl oz/1 cup)* **stout**

60 ml *(2 fl oz/¼ cup)* **malt vinegar**

250 ml *(9 fl oz/1 cup)* **chicken stock**

1 tablespoon **brown sugar**

steamed greens > *to serve*

1 · · · Preheat the oven to 160°C (315°F). Heat the oil in a flameproof, heavy-based casserole dish over high heat. Cook the lamb, skin side down, for 5 minutes, or until the fat is golden brown. Turn over and cook for another 5 minutes.

2 · · · Strew the onion, garlic, rosemary and bay leaf over the lamb, then season well with sea salt and freshly ground black pepper. Use a large spoon or tongs to push the ingredients around in the pan, so the onion starts to sizzle in the oil. Cook for 5 minutes, or until the onion smells sweet and just starts to colour.

3 · · · Add the stout, vinegar, stock and sugar. Give the pan a shake to loosen any bits that are stuck. Turn the lamb over a couple of times so the ingredients are well combined.

4 · · · Cover with a tight-fitting lid, then transfer to the oven and bake for 2½–3 hours, or until the lamb easily pulls away from the bone. Remove from the oven, leave to rest for a while, then serve with steamed greens.

I didn't really plan it this way, but there is a plethora of <u>gluten-free</u> recipes in this chapter. (Nice one for the coeliacs.) A better-than-decent, gluten-free beer is naturally crafted <u>O'Brien Premium Lager</u>. This beer brand has a cute gimmick — a beer for every season. Check it out.

IRISH STEW

This is a truly minimal recipe. With so few ingredients, you could wonder how it's all going to end up. I've seen other versions of this recipe that throw in every vegetable on hand: leeks, carrots, celery and parsnips. But I've kept this pared back to its purest form — meat, potato and onion, with the only 'fancy' ingredient being parsley. The lamb neck is a mostly underused cut of meat, but yields so much flavour. A dark ale is definitely the drink of choice here.

SERVES **4**

1 kg *(2 lb 4 oz)* **lamb neck**

2 **onions** > *thinly sliced into rings*

750 g *(1 lb 10 oz)* **firm, waxy potatoes** > *cut into 5 mm (¼ inch) slices*

10 g *(¼ oz/¼ cup)* **chopped flat-leaf** *(Italian)* **parsley**

250 ml *(9 fl oz/1 cup)* **beef stock**

1 ⋯ **Preheat the oven to 160°C (315°F). Season the lamb with sea salt and freshly ground black pepper. Put about a quarter of the lamb in a casserole dish. Add a quarter each of the onion, potato and parsley, then season well. Repeat to use up all the lamb, onion, potato and parsley.**

2 ⋯ **Pour the stock over the ingredients. Cover the dish, then transfer to the oven and bake for 3 hours. By this time, all the ingredients will be fork-tender.**

This is a super-rich Polish stew, also known as bigos. There are a few other European versions of the same dish — the Italians, for instance, have their own — but, for me, this is the richest. It is guaranteed to leave any belly full and sated on a cold (Polish) day... especially when enjoyed with a stout or two.

S
E
R
V
E
S

4

220 g *(7¾ oz/1 cup)* **pitted prunes**

8–10 **dried porcini mushrooms** > *sliced*

2 tablespoons **butter**

1 **onion** > *chopped*

½ teaspoon **sea salt**

250 g *(9 oz)* **Polish smoked sausage** > *chopped*

250 g *(9 oz)* **bratwurst or pork and garlic sausages** > *chopped*

500 g *(1 lb 2 oz)* **pork neck** > *cut into 4 cm (1½ inch) chunks*

250 ml *(9 fl oz/1 cup)* **dry red wine**

½ **red cabbage** > *finely shredded*

150 g *(5½ oz/1 cup)* **ready-made sauerkraut**

400 g *(14 oz)* tin **chopped tomatoes**

1 **bay leaf**

¼ teaspoon **freshly ground black pepper**

boiled small potatoes > *to serve*

1 · · · **Put the prunes and mushrooms in a heatproof bowl. Pour over 250 ml (9 fl oz/1 cup) boiling water and leave for 30 minutes, or until the mushrooms have softened. Drain well, reserving the liquid. Roughly chop and set aside.**

2 · · · **Preheat the oven to 160°C (315°F). Heat the butter in a flameproof heavy-based casserole dish over medium–high heat. Add the onion and salt and cook for 2–3 minutes, or until the onion has softened.**

3 · · · **Add the sausages and cook for a few minutes, until the raw meat is brown. Add the pork and cook for 8–10 minutes, stirring often, until brown all over.**

4 · · · **Now add the wine and cabbage, stirring to remove any bits stuck to the bottom of the pan. Cook for about 10 minutes, or until the wine has reduced by about half and the cabbage is soft.**

5 · · · **Stir in the sauerkraut, tomatoes, bay leaf, pepper, prunes, mushrooms and the reserved soaking liquid. Stir to combine and bring to the boil. Cover, then transfer to the oven and bake for 2 hours. Serve with boiled potatoes.**

PORK
BRAISED IN MILK

This is a not uncommon way to cook pork in Italy, Mexico, and Central and South America. The milk cooks away to nothing more than sugars and protein, rendering the pork sweet, fork-tender, and fragrant with the spices. The braised pork is also wonderful pulled into shreds and served in taco shells with shredded iceberg lettuce, coriander (cilantro) and lime juice. Lovely with a lager.

1 tablespoon **vegetable oil**

1 kg *(2 lb 4 oz)* **boneless pork shoulder** > *cut into 4 cm (1½ inch) chunks*

½ teaspoon **sea salt**

1 teaspoon **dried oregano**

1 stick **cinnamon**

1 **bay leaf**

1 teaspoon **ground black pepper**

1 **orange** > *cut in half*

500 ml *(17 fl oz/2 cups)* **milk**

steamed broccolini > *to serve*

SERVES **4**

1 · · · **Preheat the oven to 180°C (350°F). Heat the oil in a flameproof heavy-based casserole dish over medium–high heat. Brown the pork pieces in two batches for about 4–5 minutes, turning often, until well browned.**

2 · · · **Return all the pork to the dish. Add the salt, oregano, cinnamon, bay leaf and pepper. Squeeze the juice from the orange halves directly into the pan, then throw in the orange halves. Stir and cook for a couple of minutes, then pour in the milk and 250 ml (9 fl oz/1 cup) water.**

3 · · · **Bring to the boil, then cover with a tight-fitting lid. Transfer to the oven and bake for 2 hours, or until the meat falls apart easily.**

4 · · · **Remove the lid, return to the oven and bake for a further 20–30 minutes, or until most of the liquid has evaporated. Remove from the oven and leave the pork in the dish to cool a little, before serving with steamed broccolini.**

LAMB SHAWARMA

*Shawarma is a way of preparing and cooking meat in the Eastern
Mediterranean, but not so far west as Arabian countries. With this method,
marinated chicken, beef or lamb is skewered and slow-cooked over a spit. Now, most
of us don't have a spit at home (if you did, you probably wouldn't need this recipe),
but surprisingly, an authentic shawarma flavour can be achieved easily enough
in your own oven. This is a dish that will easily stand up to a dark ale.*

1 **boned lamb leg** > *about 2 kg (4 lb 8 oz)* > *skin on*

flatbread, salad leaves, yoghurt and lemon wedges > *to serve*

SERVES 4

SPICE PASTE

2 tablespoons **ground cumin**

2 teaspoons **black peppercorns**

1 **cinnamon stick** > *broken into small pieces*

1 tablespoon **sweet paprika**

2 teaspoons **ground ginger**

1 tablespoon **sea salt**

1 bunch **coriander** *(cilantro)* > *finely chopped*

2 **garlic cloves** > *finely chopped*

60 ml *(2 fl oz/¼ cup)* **olive oil**

1 · · · Start by making the spice paste. Heat a small frying pan over high heat.
Add the cumin, peppercorns and cinnamon. Shake the pan and cook for just
a few seconds, until the spices smoke and pop.

2 · · · Tip into a bowl and stir in the paprika, ginger and salt. Allow to cool,
then grind the spices to a rough powder, using a spice mill or a mortar and
pestle. Stir in the coriander, garlic and oil to make a paste. Rub the paste
all over the lamb and refrigerate for 6 hours, or overnight.

3 · · · Preheat the oven to 220°C (425°F). Sit the lamb, skin side up, in a roasting
tin. Roast for 20 minutes, by which time the spice rub will be aromatic.

4 · · · Add 250 ml (9 fl oz/1 cup) cold water to the tin, pouring it all around the
lamb, not over it (you don't want to wash off the seasonings). Cover the tin
firmly with a couple of layers of foil. Turn the oven down to 150°C (300°F)
and bake for 4 hours, or until the lamb is fall-apart tender.

5 · · · Remove the lamb from the oven. Leave covered for 20–30 minutes, to rest
and cool slightly. Shred the lamb using tongs or forks, or serve it in large chunks,
wrapped in flatbread, with salad leaves, yoghurt and lemon wedges.

COWBOY CHILLI

The end result here resembles a rich, chocolate-coloured Indian beef curry. The look of it sets the tone for the flavours to follow — warmly spiced and a little sweet from the dark beer and tomatoes. Serve with small, soft tortillas to wrap the odd bit of meat in, and a hearty stout.

SERVES **4**

2 tablespoons **vegetable oil**

1 **large onion** > *sliced into wedges*

2 **garlic cloves** > *chopped*

750 g *(1 lb 10 oz)* **chuck steak** > *cut into 2 cm (¾ inch) chunks*

1 tablespoon **ground cumin**

1 tablespoon **hot paprika**

1 teaspoon **cayenne pepper**

1 teaspoon **dried oregano**

1 **jalapeño chilli** > *seeded and chopped*

1 **bay leaf**

400 g *(14 oz)* tin **chopped tomatoes**

400 ml *(14 fl oz)* **beef stock**

250 ml *(9 fl oz/1 cup)* **dark Mexican beer**

soft tortillas, sour cream, spring onion *(scallion)* **and coriander** *(cilantro)* > *to serve*

1 · · · Heat the oil in a heavy-based saucepan over high heat. Add the onion and garlic and cook for 2–3 minutes, until the onion starts to char around the edges.

2 · · · Add the beef chunks and stir them around in the pan to separate. Cook for 2–3 minutes, or until the meat is brown and the onion starts to almost smell burnt (as if it were being barbecued).

3 · · · Add the cumin, paprika, cayenne pepper, oregano and chilli, stirring to coat the meat in the spices. Cook for 1 minute, or until the spices are aromatic.

4 · · · Add the bay leaf, tomatoes, stock and beer, stirring to remove any bits stuck to the bottom of the pan. Bring to the boil, then reduce the heat to low. Cover and simmer for 1 hour 15 minutes.

5 · · · Remove the lid and increase the heat to high. Boil for 10–15 minutes, stirring often, until the liquid has thickened and the beef is very tender. Serve with tortillas, sour cream, spring onion slices and coriander.

F
+
B

BEER

Tex Mex food is logically paired with pale American lagers — but comfort food deserves a comfort beer. Food spiced with warming and aromatic flavours can complete and complement a malty, well-hopped <u>porter beer</u>. With toffee, caramel and chocolate tones, this is a beer to tame and flatter spicy flavours. It is said that porter was popular with transport workers in London, hence the name. Its popularity has waxed and waned, but has seen a comeback with the micro-brewing trend of the last few decades. <u>Porters</u> can be very rich and robust. A great winter beer to have with some warming winter food.

VEAL SCHNITZELS WITH SPAGHETTI MARINARA

This is a real Australian pub-grub staple. I had always been unsure of this odd combo, but like most of our favourite dishes, this has history. Pairing schnitzel with pasta is not uncommon in Swiss cooking, and several of my Italian Aussie friends inform me that their Italian nonnas would often prepare veal and spaghetti to be eaten as a meal. A nice lager will bring it all together.

SERVES **4**

300 g *(10½ oz)* **spaghetti**

finely grated parmesan cheese and lemon wedges > *to serve*

MARINARA SAUCE

2 tablespoons **olive oil**

1 **onion** > *finely chopped*

2 **garlic cloves** > *finely chopped*

6–8 **basil leaves** > *roughly torn*

60 ml *(2 fl oz/¼ cup)* **red wine**

400 g *(14 oz)* tin **chopped tomatoes**

1 tablespoon **tomato paste** *(concentrated purée)*

VEAL SCHNITZELS

2 **eggs**

2 tablespoons **milk**

2 tablespoons **plain** *(all-purpose)* **flour**

½ teaspoon **sea salt**

¼ teaspoon **ground white pepper**

200 g *(7 oz/2 cups)* **dry breadcrumbs**

4 **veal schnitzel steaks** > *about 150 g (5½ oz) each*

vegetable oil > *for frying*

1 · · · To make the marinara sauce, heat the oil in a saucepan over high heat and cook the onion for 4–5 minutes, stirring often, until softened. Add the garlic and basil and stir for a couple of minutes. Add the wine and let it sizzle and boil, then add the tomatoes, tomato paste, and a pinch each of sugar, sea salt and freshly ground black pepper. Reduce the heat and simmer for about 5 minutes, or until thickened slightly. Remove from the heat and leave for 1–3 hours, to let the flavours develop.

2 · · · Preheat the oven to 160°C (315°F). Line a baking tray with baking paper. To make the schnitzels, beat the eggs and milk in a bowl. Combine the flour, salt and pepper on one plate, and put the breadcrumbs on another plate.

3 · · · Working with one portion at a time, toss the veal in the flour, making sure each piece is coated evenly all over. Pick up the veal at one end and flap it around in the egg wash to coat all over in egg, then press into the breadcrumbs. Leave the schnitzels on the baking tray while heating the oil.

4 · · · Pour enough oil into a frying pan to come halfway up the side of the pan. Heat over medium–high heat. The oil is ready for frying when the surface of the oil is shimmering.

5 · · · Using tongs, hold a piece of veal at one end, dip it into the oil and move it around in the pan, so it doesn't stick to the pan. Add another piece of veal if there's room, but don't overcrowd the pan. Cook the veal for just 2–3 minutes on each side, until the crumbs are golden brown. Transfer to the baking tray while cooking the remaining veal, then place in the oven while cooking the spaghetti.

6 · · · Gently reheat the marinara sauce over low heat. Meanwhile, cook the spaghetti in a saucepan of lightly salted boiling water for 10–12 minutes, or until al dente. Drain well and return to the pan. Add the marinara sauce, using tongs to gently coat the spaghetti with the sauce.

7 · · · Divide the schnitzels and spaghetti among warmed plates. Scatter the spaghetti with parmesan and serve with lemon wedges.

VEAL SCHNITZELS WITH SPAGHETTI MARINARA

PULLED PORK

Say it's a Sunday morning. You put this in the oven at 10am and then get on with whatever you do on a Sunday morning. You invite some friends over, grab a few bread rolls, whip up a simple coleslaw and use this pulled pork to make the best Sunday sandwich ever, then just kick back with a relaxing stout or dark ale.

1.5 kg *(3 lb 5 oz)* **pork neck**

8 **soft bread rolls**

coleslaw and barbecue sauce > *to serve*

SERVES **8**

SPICE RUB

2 tablespoons **smoked paprika**

2 tablespoons **ground cumin**

2 tablespoons **soft brown sugar**

1 tablespoon **sea salt**

1 · · · **Preheat the oven to 220°C (425°F). Combine all the spice rub ingredients in a bowl. Roll the pork around in the bowl to evenly coat it all in the spices. Place the pork in a roasting tin and pour in 250 ml (9 fl oz/1 cup) cold water.**

2 · · · **Transfer to the oven and bake for 40 minutes; depending on the size of your roasting tin, you may need to add more water to stop the spice mix burning.**

3 · · · **Remove the roasting tin from the oven and pour in another 250 ml (9 fl oz/1 cup) water. Cover the roasting tin with foil, making sure the edges are well sealed, and bake the pork for a further 2½ hours. Remove the roasting tin from the oven and leave it covered for about 1 hour.**

4 · · · **Remove the foil, then use cooking tongs to shred the pork meat, reserving the cooking liquid. Place the shredded pork in a bowl and pour the cooking juices all over the pork. Serve on soft rolls, with coleslaw and barbecue sauce.**

CUBAN SANDWICH

This one incites passion. Purists call for traditional, sweet Cuban bread, similar to French or Italian bread — but sliced sourdough or baguette will do. The braised pork is also great wrapped in a soft, warm burrito with some Guacamole (page 27), iceberg lettuce and coriander (cilantro) sprigs. Glorious with a golden ale.

SERVES **4**

1 **long baguette** > *halved lengthways and cut into 4 pieces*

2 tablespoons **dijon mustard**

8 thin slices **Swiss cheese**

150 g *(5½ oz/1 cup)* **bread and butter pickles**

8 thin slices **ham**

BRAISED PORK

2 tablespoons **extra virgin olive oil**

60 ml *(2 fl oz/¼ cup)* **orange juice**

60 ml *(2 fl oz/¼ cup)* **lime juice**

4 **garlic cloves** > *crushed*

1 tablespoon **dried oregano**

1 tablespoon **ground cumin**

¼ teaspoon **chilli flakes**

1 teaspoon **sea salt**

½ teaspoon **ground black pepper**

1 kg *(2 lb 4 oz)* **pork shoulder**

1 · · · **To braise the pork, combine the oil, orange juice, lime juice, garlic, oregano and spices in a large bowl. Add the pork and tumble the meat around to coat in the mixture. Cover and set aside for 30 minutes, or refrigerate for 3–6 hours.**

2 · · · **Preheat the oven to 220°C (425°F). Transfer the pork and all the marinade to a roasting tin. Add 125 ml (4 fl oz/½ cup) water and roast for 30 minutes.**

3 · · · **Turn the oven down to 170°C (325°F). Tightly cover the roasting tin with foil, then bake for a further 3–3½ hours. Remove from the oven and allow the pork to rest for 30 minutes to 1 hour.**

4 · · · **Shred the pork. Spread the baguette halves with mustard, then fill with layers of shredded pork, cheese, pickles and ham. Cook the sandwiches, using a sandwich press, until the bread is golden and crisp, or wrap in foil and bake in a preheated 180°C (350°F) oven for 10 minutes. Cut into slices to serve.**

GOULASH

The national dish of Hungary, goulash lies somewhere between a soup and a stew, and reminds me of the Moroccan lamb dish, harira. But don't get me wrong. Goulash has no identity crisis. It knows exactly what it is: a hearty, comforting staple with more than a hint of warming, spicy paprika and caraway, the latter being a flavour that goes hand in hand with cold climates — and a dark ale!

SERVES 4

1 tablespoon **butter**

2 **red onions** > *chopped*

3 **garlic cloves** > *chopped*

2 **green bullhorn chillies** > *seeded and thinly sliced*

1 kg *(2 lb 4 oz)* **beef shin** > *cut into 4 cm (1½ inch) chunks*

4 tablespoons **sweet paprika**

1 teaspoon **caraway seeds**

400 g *(14 oz)* tin **chopped tomatoes**

sour cream and chopped flat-leaf *(Italian)* **parsley** > *to serve*

1 ··· Heat the butter in a flameproof heavy-based casserole dish over medium heat. Add the onion, garlic and chilli and cook for 5–6 minutes, stirring often, until the onion has softened.

2 ··· Add the beef, mixing the onion through. Stir in the paprika and caraway seeds to thickly coat the meat in the aromatic spices. Cook for 8–10 minutes, stirring often, until the meat is browning nicely. Season well with sea salt and freshly ground black pepper.

3 ··· Stir the tomatoes through and add about 250 ml (9 fl oz/1 cup) water, stirring to remove any bits stuck to the bottom of the dish. Bring to the boil over high heat, then reduce the heat to low. Cover with a tight-fitting lid and cook for 1½ hours, stirring only every now and then. Serve dolloped with sour cream and garnished with parsley.

STUFFED CABBAGE LEAVES

I've tried these many times and in many ways. One method I tried was cooking the meat prior to rolling it up in cabbage leaves, but this was crumbly, difficult to eat, and the meat not so tasty. Leaving the meat uncooked, with all the other bits, produces a really firmly packed roll that is easy to eat and bursting with fabulous flavours. A wheat beer will help bring it all home.

½ **cabbage** > *untrimmed*

110 g *(3¾ oz/½ cup)* **short-grain rice**

500 g *(1 lb 2 oz)* **minced** *(ground)* **pork**

2 **garlic cloves** > *finely chopped*

small handful **flat-leaf** *(Italian)* **parsley** > *finely chopped*

1 teaspoon **caraway seeds**

1 teaspoon **chilli flakes**

2 **onions** > *finely chopped*

2 teaspoons **dried dill tips**

1 tablespoon **sweet paprika**

60 ml *(2 fl oz/¼ cup)* **olive oil**

500 ml *(17 fl oz/2 cups)* **tomato passata** *(puréed tomatoes)*

250 ml *(9 fl oz/1 cup)* **chicken stock**

sour cream and chopped fresh dill > *to serve*

SERVES 4

1 · · · Bring a large saucepan of salted water to the boil. Tear off and discard any tough outer leaves from the cabbage. Holding the cabbage by the stem end, place it in the saucepan. Cover the pan and turn the heat off.

2 · · · Leave the cabbage in the pot for 10 minutes. Now carefully tip the pot of water and the cabbage into a clean sink, then leave the cabbage there to cool.

3 · · · Cook the rice in a saucepan of boiling water for 10 minutes. Drain well, then tip into a bowl. Add the pork, garlic, parsley, caraway seeds and chilli flakes, along with half the onion, half the dill and half the paprika. Season with sea salt and freshly ground black pepper. Use your hands to squeeze the mixture together until sausage- or paste-like. Divide into six equal portions.

4 · · · Cut about 5 cm (2 inches) off the stem end of the cabbage and discard. Gently pull the leaves off the cabbage, being careful not to tear them. You will need six large leaves.

5 · · · Use a sharp knife to make a V-shaped cut to remove the thick part of the stem in the middle of the leaves. Discard the stemmy bits. Use several of the remaining leaves to line the base of a baking dish.

6 · · · Lay a cabbage leaf on a clean work surface. Put a portion of pork in the centre of the leaf and form into a sausage shape. Roll the cabbage leaf over the pork, tucking in the sides to firmly enclose the filling. Repeat to make six cabbage rolls, then place in the baking dish.

7 · · · Preheat the oven to 160°C (315°F). Heat the oil in a frying pan over medium–high heat. Add the remaining onion and cook for 5–6 minutes, or until soft. Stir in the remaining dill and paprika and cook for just 1 minute, or until fragrant.

8 · · · Add the tomato passata and stock and season well. Bring to the boil for a couple of minutes, then pour over the cabbage. Cover the dish with a tight-fitting lid, transfer to the oven and bake for 2 hours. Serve with sour cream and dill.

STUFFED CABBAGE LEAVES

STROGANOFF

Here's a fun and easy classic for kitchen novices. Its flavours will always be good, but its simplicity calls for great attention to the ingredients and the method. Or rather, the method dictates the ingredients, and insists that you use the finest-quality lean beef fillet here, as the meat is lightly pan-fried, then ever so gently poached in the sauce for only a few minutes. The whole thing — mushrooms, sauce and beef — should just melt in your mouth. Enjoy with stout or schwarzbier.

500 g *(1 lb 2 oz)* **beef eye fillet**

2 tablespoons **plain** *(all-purpose)* **flour**

¼ teaspoon **ground allspice**

50 g *(1¾ oz)* **butter**

1 **onion** > *thinly sliced*

500 g *(1 lb 2 oz)* **mushrooms** > *thinly sliced*

125 ml *(4 fl oz/½ cup)* **beef stock**

2 tablespoons **tomato paste** *(concentrated purée)*

125 g *(4½ oz/½ cup)* **sour cream**

tagliatelle or other wide egg pasta > *to serve*

SERVES **4**

1 · · · Cut the beef into 1 cm (½ inch) thick pieces, then slice into strips. Place on a plate, sprinkle with the flour and allspice, then season with sea salt and freshly ground black pepper. Rub the flour mixture all over the beef.

2 · · · Heat half the butter in a frying pan over high heat. Depending on the size of the pan, you may need to work in batches here. Add the beef to the pan in one layer and cook for just 1 minute on each side. The meat will be slightly coloured and pink around the sides. Put the browned beef on a plate, then repeat with the remaining beef if necessary.

3 · · · Add the remaining butter to the pan, along with the onion. Reduce the heat to medium and cook for 5–6 minutes, or until the onion is golden and sweet-smelling. Add the mushrooms and cook for 15 minutes, stirring often, until they have collapsed and are tender and aromatic.

4 · · · Pour the stock into the pan, stirring to remove any bits that are stuck. Allow to cook for a couple of minutes. Stir in the tomato paste, then the sour cream, until well combined and smooth and creamy.

5 · · · Now add the beef and any juices. Reduce the heat to low and gently simmer for 1–2 minutes; any longer will render the beef tough. Serve with pasta.

<u>Schwarzbier</u> *(pronounced shvarts-beer)* simply translates as 'black beer'. Not as heavy or bitter as porters or stouts, and lacking dominant flavours such as chocolate and roasted malt, a good black beer should have a perfect combination of lightness and sweetness — sometimes described as creamy. With a black beer, you could sit down to a meal of good cheese and bread. Or better yet, a fine stroganoff!

SHAKING BEEF

Another fabulously tasty Vietnamese recipe. I'd eat this with the Tomato rice (page 223) and sliced fresh tomato and cucumber. Using good-quality, very lean beef is essential: the cooking time is so fast that any fat won't have time to render away or tenderise, and the meat will be tough. Also, you really need to get your pan or wok fiery hot. If you feel your cooktop won't be hot enough (like mine!), this is a good recipe to take outside and cook on the barbecue, with a lager.

SERVES

4

2 tablespoons **fish sauce**

1 tablespoon **oyster sauce**

2 **garlic cloves** > *very finely chopped*

3 tablespoons **sugar**

500 g *(1 lb 2 oz)* **beef fillet** > *cut into 2 cm (¾ inch) cubes*

125 ml *(4 fl oz/½ cup)* **rice vinegar**

1 teaspoon **sea salt**

2 tablespoons **vegetable oil**

Tomato rice (page 223), sliced cucumber, tomato and lime wedges > *to serve*

DIPPING SAUCE

80 ml *(2½ fl oz/⅓ cup)* **lime juice**

½ teaspoon **ground white pepper**

1 teaspoon **sugar**

¹ ··· In a bowl, combine the fish sauce, oyster sauce, garlic and 1 tablespoon of the sugar. Add the beef cubes and stir them around in the sauce, so the meat is evenly coated. Cover and set aside for 1–2 hours; during this time the beef will darken.

² ··· In a small bowl, combine the remaining 2 tablespoons sugar with the rice vinegar and salt; set aside. Combine the dipping sauce ingredients in a small serving bowl and set aside.

³ ··· Heat the oil in a frying pan over high heat. Swirl the pan to coat in the oil. Tip the beef and any marinade into the hot pan in one layer. Cook, without turning or moving, for 2–3 minutes. Then start to shake the pan to remove any pieces of beef stuck to the bottom.

⁴ ··· Add the rice vinegar mixture and shake the pan vigorously, to coat the meat. Serve with tomato rice and dipping sauce, with some cucumber, tomato and lime wedges on the side.

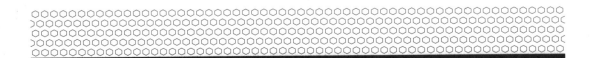

CARAMEL PORK HOTPOT

Cooking food in unglazed clay pots is common in Vietnam and China. These pots can be picked up at Asian speciality stores and need to be treated before using. To treat a clay pot, soak it in cold water for several hours, then put the empty pot in a warm oven for a couple of hours until completely dry. The pot can then be placed directly on a hotplate. Wonderfully sweet, dark and fragrant, this pork hotpot is begging to be washed down with a wheat beer.

60 ml *(2 fl oz/¼ cup)* **vegetable oil or light peanut oil**

500 g *(1 lb 2 oz)* **pork loin** > *cut into 3 cm (1¼ inch) cubes*

70 g *(2½ oz/½ cup)* **palm sugar** *(jaggery)* > *finely chopped*

4 **spring onions** *(scallions)* > *cut into 3 cm (1¼ inch) lengths*

4 **garlic cloves** > *roughly chopped*

5 cm *(2 inch)* chunk **fresh ginger** > *peeled and sliced*

125 ml *(4 fl oz/½ cup)* **fish sauce**

½ teaspoon **ground white pepper**

coriander *(cilantro)* **sprigs and steamed jasmine rice** > *to serve*

SERVES 4

1 · · · Preheat the oven to 160°C (315°F). Heat the oil in a clay pot or a small heavy-based saucepan over high heat. Add several cubes of pork and cook for 2–3 minutes, or until golden. Remove to a plate. Allow the oil to reheat and for any water to sizzle away. Cook the remaining pork, then remove from the pot.

2 · · · Add the palm sugar to the pot. Use metal tongs or a large metal spoon to stir the sugar so it dissolves in the oil. Let the sugar cook in the hot oil and it will start to froth up and bubble, a bit like toffee. Let it cook like this for 1 minute without burning.

3 · · · Add the spring onion, garlic and ginger to the pot. Stir a few times to separate the ingredients so they cook evenly. Cook for 1 minute, just to soften.

4 · · · Stir in the fish sauce, pepper and 125 ml (4 fl oz/½ cup) water. Return the pork to the pot and give it a good stir. Bring to the boil, then put the lid on. Transfer to the oven and bake for 1½ hours, or until the pork is sweet, dark and tender. Serve with coriander and jasmine rice.

VEAL CORDON BLEU

You could buy veal tenderloins and pound them into thinner pieces, or buy the veal prepared as thin schnitzels, ready to cook. I suggest the latter for this recipe. Either way, you want a piece of veal no thicker than 5 mm (¼ inch), and about 20 cm (8 inches) long and 10 cm (4 inches) wide. A bit of a process here, but make them in advance for a dinner gathering and keep them in the fridge. Cooked just before you're ready to eat, these will impress — especially with a hearty stout.

4 **veal schnitzel steaks** > *about 150 g (5½ oz) each*	S E R V E S **4**
4 slices **good-quality ham**	
4 slices **Swiss cheese**	
150 g *(5½ oz/1 cup)* **plain** *(all-purpose)* **flour**	
ground white pepper > *for seasoning*	
3 **eggs**	
60 ml *(2 fl oz/¼ cup)* **milk**	
200 g *(7 oz/2 cups)* **dry breadcrumbs**	
250 ml *(9 fl oz/1 cup)* **vegetable oil** > *for frying*	
1 tablespoon **butter**	
lemon wedges > *to serve*	

1 · · · Using a sharp knife, slice each piece of veal in half horizontally. Lay four veal halves on a chopping board. Put a piece of ham and cheese on each piece, then lay another piece of veal on top. Season with sea salt and freshly ground black pepper and press around the edges to seal.

2 · · · Pour the flour onto a plate and season with sea salt and ground white pepper. In a bowl, whisk together the eggs and milk. Put the breadcrumbs on another plate.

3 · · · Press both sides of the veal parcels into the flour, dip them in the egg mix, then press into the breadcrumbs.

4 · · · Heat the oil and butter in a large heavy-based frying pan over medium heat. When the butter has melted and is sizzling in the oil, add two veal parcels. Cook for 4–5 minutes on each side, or until golden brown.

5 · · · Remove the cooked veal to a plate, cover with foil and keep warm while cooking the remaining veal. Serve with lemon wedges.

GRANDMA'S PORK AND TOFU

This dish, called ma po dofu, apparently means 'pock-marked grandmother'. 'Ants climbing trees' (page 214) is another recipe in this book exemplifying the Chinese penchant for incongruous names. While its name may not be the most appealing, this flavoursome dish certainly is. Round it all out with a dark ale.

SERVES **4**

300 g *(10½ oz)* **minced** *(ground)* **pork**

1 tablespoon **light soy sauce**

1 tablespoon **Chinese rice wine**

1 teaspoon **cornflour** *(cornstarch)*

½ teaspoon **sea salt**

400 g *(14 oz)* **soft tofu** > *cut into 2 cm (¾ inch) cubes*

60 ml *(2 fl oz/¼ cup)* **vegetable or light peanut oil**

2 **garlic cloves** > *finely chopped*

1 tablespoon **fresh ginger** > *finely chopped*

2 **spring onions** *(scallions)* > *finely chopped*

1 tablespoon **salted fermented black beans** > *smashed with a fork*

1 tablespoon **chilli paste**

steamed rice > *to serve*

SAUCE

60 ml *(2 fl oz/¼ cup)* **chicken stock**

1 tablespoon **light soy sauce**

1 teaspoon **cornflour** *(cornstarch)*

1 ··· Combine the pork, soy sauce, rice wine, cornflour and salt in a bowl and set aside. Bring a small saucepan of water to the boil. Add a pinch of salt and the tofu. Remove from the heat and allow the tofu to steep in the water until needed.

2 ··· Heat a wok over high heat. Add the oil and swirl the wok to coat in the oil. Add the garlic, ginger and spring onion and stir-fry for just a few seconds, or until softened and aromatic. Add the pork and stir-fry for 4–5 minutes, or until well combined, breaking up any clumps. Stir the black beans and chilli paste through, then simmer for 2–3 minutes, until the juices are a chilli-red colour.

3 ··· Combine the sauce ingredients in a small bowl. Drain the tofu. Add the sauce to the wok, then gently stir in the tofu. Gently simmer until the sauce coats the pork and tofu. Remove the wok from the heat, cover and leave to sit while you steam your rice. During this time all the flavours will meld beautifully.

SWEET AND SOUR PORK

My dad, a huge fan of Chinese cookery, makes the best version of this Cantonese classic. The marinade is also the batter and works like magic. The first thing one is taught in cooking Chinese food is to be prepared: always have all the ingredients ready to go, portioned out in bowls. When all the action is over, settle back with a cooling pilsener or lager.

600 g *(1 lb 5 oz)* **pork scotch fillet** > *cut into 2 cm (¾ inch) chunks*

1 tablespoon **Chinese rice wine**

1 tablespoon **light soy sauce**

2 teaspoons **sesame oil**

2 **egg yolks**

1 teaspoon **cornflour** *(cornstarch)*

½ teaspoon **sea salt**

110 g *(3¾ oz/¾ cup)* **plain** *(all-purpose)* **flour**

500 ml *(17 fl oz/2 cups)* **light peanut oil**

1 **small red capsicum** *(pepper)* > *thinly sliced*

1 **small green capsicum** *(pepper)* > *thinly sliced*

1 **small carrot** > *cut into thin matchsticks*

1 **large red chilli** > *thinly sliced*

2 **garlic cloves** > *chopped*

1 tablespoon **fresh ginger** > *thinly shredded*

steamed jasmine rice > *to serve*

SERVES 4

SAUCE

1 tablespoon **tomato paste** *(concentrated purée)*

55 g *(2 oz/¼ cup)* **white sugar**

185 ml *(6 fl oz/¾ cup)* **white vinegar**

2 tablespoons **light soy sauce**

1 teaspoon **cornflour** *(cornstarch)*

[1] ··· Put the pork in a bowl that is the right size to fit it all snugly. Add the rice wine, soy sauce, sesame oil, egg yolks, cornflour and salt. Mix it all together; I find the best way is to use your hands, but you could use a fork or chopsticks if you prefer. Cover and refrigerate for 3–6 hours, or even overnight.

[2] ··· When ready to cook, stir the plain flour through the pork so the pork is coated in a thick, sticky batter. Combine the sauce ingredients in a bowl and set aside.

[3] ··· Heat the peanut oil in a wok or saucepan over high heat. The oil is ready when the surface is shimmering. Using chopsticks or metal tongs, add several pieces of the battered pork to the oil and fry for 2–3 minutes, or until golden. Remove to a plate. Give the oil a little time to reheat and cook the remaining pork in batches.

[4] ··· Pour off all but about 1 tablespoon of oil from the wok. Add the capsicums, carrot, chilli, garlic and ginger and stir-fry for 3–4 minutes, or until the vegetables are tender but still crisp.

[5] ··· Add the sauce mixture to the wok, stir thoroughly and cook for 2–3 minutes to allow the mixture to boil and thicken. Return the pork to the wok and stir together well. Serve with steamed jasmine rice.

SWEET AND SOUR PORK

BEEF AND GUINNESS STEW

This dish exemplifies the alchemy of slow cooking. There aren't many ingredients, and your shopping list is about as basic it can get. Speck is basically a smoked slab of the tail end of bacon. It may be a challenge to hunt down, but I probably wouldn't suggest replacing it with anything else. If you can't find speck, just leave it out — the recipe will still hit the spot. And so will a stout.

350 g (12 oz) piece **smoked speck** > *skin on*

1 **onion** > *thinly sliced*

1 **carrot** > *diced*

1 **celery stalk** > *diced*

500 g *(1 lb 2 oz)* **chuck steak** > *cut into 3 cm (1¼ inch) chunks*

440 ml *(15¼ fl oz/1¾ cups)* **Guinness**

250 ml *(9 fl oz/1 cup)* **beef stock**

1 **bay leaf**

3 tablespoons **flat-leaf** *(Italian)* **parsley** > *finely chopped*

2 tablespoons **plain** *(all-purpose)* **flour**

creamy mashed potatoes > *to serve*

1 ··· Remove the skin from the speck, leaving some of the fat on. Cut the meat into large dice. Heat a heavy-based frying pan over high heat, add the speck and cook for 8–10 minutes, stirring to brown all over and render the fat.

2 ··· Add the onion and cook for 2–3 minutes, stirring to separate all the slices. Add the carrot and celery and stir-fry for a couple of minutes, so that all the ingredients are combined and coated in the tasty bacon fat.

3 ··· Add the beef and stir it around in the pan until it just starts to colour. Pour in 375 ml (13 fl oz/1½ cups) of the Guinness and let the beer simmer for 4–5 minutes, stirring to remove any bits stuck to the bottom of the pan.

4 ··· Add the stock, bay leaf and parsley. Reduce the heat to low, so the liquid is gently simmering. Cover and cook for 1½ hours, stirring after about 1 hour.

5 ··· Remove the lid and increase the heat to high, allowing the sauce to boil. Mix the remaining Guinness with the flour to make a smooth paste, then stir it into the stew and cook until the sauce thickens. Season to taste with sea salt and freshly ground black pepper. Serve with mashed potatoes.

SLOW-COOKED BEEF SHIN WITH RADISH

Beef shin is a cut of meat we don't really see often, except on menus in some Chinese restaurants. Here it is cooked in what could be described as a classic red braise — a Chinese method of slow-cooking meat in a mixture of soy sauce, rice wine and aromatics. A stout is the beer to do this rich dish justice.

SERVES **4**

1 kg *(2 lb 4 oz)* **beef shin** > *about 4 pieces*

1 tablespoon **vegetable oil**

5 **garlic cloves** > *crushed*

5 cm *(2 inch)* chunk **fresh ginger** > *thinly sliced*

125 ml *(4 fl oz/½ cup)* **rice wine**

250 ml *(9 fl oz/1 cup)* **dark soy sauce**

125 ml *(4 fl oz/½ cup)* **oyster sauce**

2 **star anise**

1 **cinnamon stick** > *broken in half*

3 **cloves**

1 tablespoon **sugar**

1 **white radish** > *peeled* > *cut into 5 cm (2 inch) pieces*

coriander *(cilantro)* **sprigs, Chinese celery leaves and white pepper** > *to serve*

1 · · · In a large saucepan, bring 2.5 litres (85 fl oz/10 cups) water to the boil. Add the beef shin, reduce the heat to low, then cover the pan and simmer for 30 minutes. Remove the beef and reserve the stock. When the beef is cool enough to handle, slice it into chunks about 2 cm (¾ inch) thick.

2 · · · Heat the oil in a heavy-based saucepan over high heat. Add the garlic and ginger and stir-fry for 1 minute, or until aromatic but not burnt. Add the rice wine and let it sizzle in the pan for 1 minute.

3 · · · Add 1.25 litres (44 fl oz/5 cups) of the reserved stock, along with the soy sauce, oyster sauce, star anise, cinnamon, cloves and sugar. Bring to the boil, then add the beef. Reduce the heat to low, then cover and simmer for 2 hours.

4 · · · Remove the lid and increase the heat to high. Stir in the radish and cook for 30 minutes, or until the radish is tender and the sauce has thickened. Serve with coriander, Chinese celery and white pepper.

I am going to suggest drinking an Irish stout with the traditional Chinese beef shin on the previous page. An odd call, but hear me out. The best-known Irish beer has to be <u>Guinness</u>, which has pleased many for over 200 years. It has an unmistakable chocolate colour, with the aroma of sweet dark soy sauce. Its hint of barley also sits nicely with the earthy radish. All in all, a lovely beer to have with such unctuous and aromatic fare.

CHAR SUI (CHINESE BBQ PORK)

I wondered about the authenticity of this recipe and how tomato sauce fits into the equation, but tomato sauce is indeed used as an alternative to red food colour in many Cantonese cookery books from the 1960s. At a pop-up Sunday yum cha I did, this item was the most popular. At yum cha, dumplings dominate the menu, or rather trollies, but don't overlook the plates of Chinese meats (duck, pork and chicken). Such delicious foods scream for a palate-cleansing, cold Asian pale or light lager.

1 kg *(2 lb 4 oz)* **pork scotch fillet**

1 tablespoon **light soy sauce**

1 tablespoon **Chinese rice wine**

1 teaspoon **sugar**

small coriander *(cilantro)* **sprigs** > *to garnish*

steamed rice and Asian greens > *to serve*

SERVES **6**

BARBECUE SAUCE

250 ml *(9 fl oz/1 cup)* **tomato sauce**

60 ml *(2 fl oz/¼ cup)* **plum sauce**

1 tablespoon **sesame oil**

220 g *(8 oz/1 cup)* **sugar**

1 teaspoon **Chinese five-spice**

¼ teaspoon **ground white pepper**

1 · · · Cut the pork lengthways into long, sausage-like fillets about 5 cm (2 inches) thick, then place in a bowl. Stir together all the barbecue sauce ingredients to dissolve the sugar, then pour over the pork. Rub the sauce into the pork, coating the meat evenly. Cover and refrigerate for 3–6 hours, or overnight.

2 · · · Preheat the oven to 220°C (425°F). Line a baking tray with baking paper. Lay the pork on the baking tray, reserving the barbecue sauce for basting.

3 · · · Roast the pork for 20 minutes, or until the edges are just starting to char. Turn and cook for another 20 minutes. Turn the oven down to 160°C (315°F) and roast for a further 2 hours, brushing with the reserved sauce and turning every 20 minutes, until the pork is very tender and deep red. Remove from the oven and set aside to rest for 30 minutes.

4 · · · Combine the soy sauce, rice wine and sugar in a bowl. Pour in 125 ml (4 fl oz/½ cup) water, stirring to dissolve the sugar.

5 · · · Slice the pork on a serving platter. Drizzle with some of the soy sauce mixture and garnish with coriander. Serve with steamed rice and Asian greens.

LAMB MACHOUI

BIGGER CRITTERS

Not to be confused with machouia, which is basically a Tunisian vegetable and chilli salad, machoui is a Northern African dish that uses intensely flavoured spices to smother slow-cooked lamb. It goes marvellously well with a wheat beer.

SERVES 4

600 g *(1 lb 5 oz)* **lamb shoulder** > *deboned and butterflied*

125 g *(4½ oz)* **unsalted butter** > *at room temperature*

½ teaspoon **sea salt**

1 tablespoon **ground cumin**

1 tablespoon **ground coriander**

1 tablespoon **sweet paprika**

flatbread and plain yoghurt > *to serve*

SPICED CUMIN SALT

¼ teaspoon **ground cumin**

½ teaspoon **chilli flakes**

2 tablespoons **sea salt**

1 ··· Preheat the oven to 220°C (425°F). Lay the lamb in a ceramic baking dish and pour 125 ml (4 fl oz/½ cup) water around it.

2 ··· Combine the butter in a bowl with the salt, cumin, coriander and paprika, mixing to make a dark-coloured paste. Smear the paste over the top of the lamb.

3 ··· Transfer to the oven and roast for 20 minutes. Turn the oven down to 160°C (315°F) and roast for a further 3 hours, or until the meat falls apart when pressed. Remove from the oven, cover with foil and allow to rest for 30 minutes.

4 ··· To make the spiced cumin salt, grind the cumin, chilli flakes and salt in a spice grinder, then tip into a small serving bowl.

5 ··· Break the meat off in large chunks and serve on flatbread, with the yoghurt and spiced cumin salt.

BURMESE BEEF CURRY

Nicknamed the Land of the Golden Pagodas, Burma is now known as Myanmar. Monks in vibrant saffron robes walk the streets, and one is never too far from the view of a pagoda, an ornamental Buddhist temple. Influenced by the cuisines of China and Thailand, the local fare abounds in simply cooked seafood, dumplings, noodles and tangy salads. Elegant colonial hotels, such as The Strand in Yangon, are the perfect place to enjoy a refreshing beverage, such as the local Myanmar Lager.

80 ml *(2½ fl oz/⅓ cup)* **vegetable oil**

1 kg *(2 lb 4 oz)* **chuck steak** > *cut into strips 1 cm (½ inch) wide*

4 **white onions** > *thinly sliced*

6 **garlic cloves** > *roughly chopped*

5 cm *(2 inch)* chunk **fresh ginger** > *peeled and grated*

2 **large red chillies** > *finely sliced on an angle*

1 tablespoon **ground turmeric**

1 teaspoon **chilli powder**

250 ml *(9 fl oz/1 cup)* **beef stock**

2 **large tomatoes** > *chopped*

1 tablespoon **light soy sauce**

large handful **coriander** *(cilantro)* > *roughly chopped*

steamed rice > *to serve*

SERVES **8**

1 ··· Heat the oil in a large, heavy-based frying pan or flameproof casserole dish over high heat. Add the beef and stir-fry for 4–5 minutes, or until the beef is just starting to brown.

2 ··· Add the onion, garlic, ginger and chilli and cook for 8–10 minutes, until the onion has collapsed and is starting to turn golden.

3 ··· Stir in the turmeric and chilli powder until well combined, then stir the stock, tomatoes and soy sauce through. Bring to the boil, then reduce the heat to a low simmer. Cover and cook for 1 hour.

4 ··· Remove the lid and cook for a further 15–30 minutes, or until the beef is tender. Stir the coriander through and serve with steamed rice.

TAGINE OF LAMB SHOULDER, POTATO AND PEAS

F+B

BIGGER CRITTERS

There are many conveniences to cooking a Moroccan-style tagine, a big one being you don't have to brown the meat first. A tagine is a one-pot wonder, with just a handful of spices (cumin, coriander, ginger and paprika) used; some recipes simply call for the top-shelf spice blend known as ras el hanout. Moroccan cooking has been described as 'Indian for beginners', but this should not be taken to imply that Moroccan cuisine is not layered and complex. I for one am a big fan, if you haven't noticed. Try a dark ale with this one.

SERVES 4

1 tablespoon **olive oil**

50 g *(1¾ oz)* **butter**

2 **onions** > *sliced into thin wedges*

3 **garlic cloves** > *chopped*

½ teaspoon **sea salt**

600 g *(1 lb 5 oz)* **lamb shoulder** > *cut into 4 cm (1½ inch) chunks*

2 teaspoons **ground cumin**

1 teaspoon **sweet paprika**

3 tablespoons **flat-leaf** *(Italian)* **parsley** > *finely chopped*

3 tablespoons **coriander** *(cilantro)* > *finely chopped*

6 **small kipfler** *(fingerling)* **potatoes** > *peeled*

pinch of **saffron threads**

155 g *(5½ oz/1 cup)* **frozen peas**

bread > *to serve*

1 ··· Heat the oil and butter in a tagine or flameproof heavy-based casserole dish over medium–high heat. When the butter is sizzling, add the onion, garlic and salt. Cook for 4–5 minutes, or until the onion has softened.

2 ··· Add the lamb pieces and stir for a couple of minutes. Sprinkle with the cumin and paprika, then stir to coat the meat in the spicy onion mixture.

3 ··· Pour in 375ml (13 fl oz/1½ cups) water, add the parsley and coriander and bring to the boil. Reduce the heat to low. Cover with a tight-fitting lid, then leave to simmer for 1½ hours.

4 ··· Meanwhile, put the potatoes and saffron in a saucepan, cover with cold water and cook over high heat until the water boils. Remove from the heat and leave for 20 minutes. Drain well.

5 ··· When the lamb has been cooking for 1½ hours, stir in the peas and lay the potatoes on top. Cover and cook for another 30 minutes. Serve with bread.

BEEF KEBABS

By day, Marrakesh's huge market place, Jemaa el Fnaa, is a bazaar selling everything from freshly squeezed orange juice with a hint of orange blossom to camel-hide handbags. At night it transforms into one giant food court, shrouded in a fug of smoke from chargrills. Beef and lamb are the meats of choice. With very little effort and expense, these beef kebabs will instantly transport you to a Moroccan marketplace. Enjoy a tall dark ale with these.

500 g *(1 lb 2 oz)* **beef rump** > *cut into 4 cm (1½ inch) chunks*

1 **onion** > *grated*

2 teaspoons **ground cumin**

2 teaspoons **hot paprika**

60 ml *(2 fl oz/¼ cup)* **olive oil**

2 tablespoons **lemon juice**

3 tablespoons **flat-leaf** *(Italian)* **parsley** > *finely chopped*

flatbread, Hummus (see page 56) and cucumber slices > *to serve*

SERVES **4**

1 · · · Put the beef, onion, spices, oil, lemon juice and parsley in a bowl. Use your hands to rub the mixture all over the beef. Cover and refrigerate for 3–6 hours, or overnight.

2 · · · Remove the beef from the fridge 30 minutes before cooking. If using wooden skewers, soak them in cold water for 30 minutes so they don't scorch during cooking.

3 · · · Heat a chargrill plate or barbecue hotplate to a high heat. Thread four or five pieces of meat onto your skewers.

4 · · · When the hotplate is smoking hot, cook the beef skewers for 4–5 minutes, then turn and cook for another 3–4 minutes. Serve with flatbread, hummus and cucumber slices.

LAMB KEFTA KEBABS

A kefta is a meatball. Having said that, you can also have kefta made with fish. Kefta can be eaten 'dry' — that is, not cooked in a sauce, but rather skewered and grilled, as we do here. Harissa (see page 57) is a must-have condiment with these kebabs, with a wheat beer or dark ale to chase it all down.

SERVES

4

1 tablespoon **olive oil**

pita bread, Hummus (page 56), **Harissa** (page 57) and **grilled lemon halves** > *to serve*

KEFTA

500 g *(1 lb 2 oz)* **minced** *(ground)* **lamb**

1 **small onion** > *grated*

3 tablespoons **coriander** *(cilantro)* > *finely chopped*

3 tablespoons **flat-leaf** *(Italian)* **parsley** > *finely chopped*

2 teaspoons **ground cumin**

1 teaspoon **hot paprika**

1 teaspoon **ground ginger**

½ teaspoon **chilli powder**

1 · · · Soak eight bamboo skewers in cold water for 30 minutes.

2 · · · Put all the kefta ingredients in a large bowl and use your hands to squeeze together well. Take handfuls of the mixture and throw them into the side of the bowl — this will tenderise the meat and give the kefta a more delicate texture.

3 · · · Divide the mixture into eight equal portions. Use wet hands to roll each into a ball, then form into an elongated oval shape about 10 cm (4 inches) long.

4 · · · Insert a soaked bambook skewer into each kefta. Place them on a tray and refrigerate for 3–6 hours, or until you want to cook them. Don't leave them for more than a day, though, and remove from the fridge 1 hour before cooking.

5 · · · Heat a chargrill plate to high. Use a brush to rub the oil all over the surface of the meat. Cook for 8 minutes, turning every 2 minutes, until evenly cooked. Serve with flatbread, hummus, harissa and grilled lemon halves.

TONKATSU

Japanese cooking is not all nori (seaweed) and omega-3s. This is the Japanese version of a schnitzel, and it can be eaten, sliced, on top of a ramen soup, or simply — as is my preference — with coleslaw, potato salad and tonkatsu sauce. The sauce recipe has many variations and is easy to make, using everyday, supermarket ingredients. Nice with grilled sausages too! And a lager, of course.

SERVES **4**

4 **pork schnitzel steaks** > *no thicker than 5 mm (¼ inch)*

ground white pepper > *for seasoning*

150 g *(5½ oz/1 cup)* **plain** *(all-purpose)* **flour**

2 **eggs**

120 g *(4¼ oz/2 cups)* **Japanese panko breadcrumbs**

vegetable oil > *for frying*

lemon wedges > *to serve*

TONKATSU SAUCE

60 ml *(2 fl oz/¼ cup)* **tomato sauce**

1 tablespoon **worcestershire sauce**

2 tablespoons **apple sauce**

1 teaspoon **mustard**

2 tablespoons **Japanese soy sauce**

2 tablespoons **malt vinegar**

¼ teaspoon **chilli powder**

1 · · · Combine the tonkatsu sauce ingredients in a bowl, or place them all in a jar and shake. Cover and store in the fridge until needed; bring back to room temperature for serving.

2 · · · Season the pork with some sea salt and ground white pepper. Pour the flour onto a plate. Beat the eggs in a bowl with 1 tablespoon water, and tip the breadcrumbs onto another plate.

3 · · · Press the pork into the flour to coat all over, dredge in the egg, then coat in the breadcrumbs.

4 · · · Pour enough oil into a frying pan to come halfway up the side of the pan. Heat over medium–high heat. The oil is ready when the surface is shimmering.

5 · · · Cook the pork in batches for 2–3 minutes, or until the crumbs are golden. Turn over and cook for another 2 minutes. Serve hot, with the tonkatsu sauce and lemon wedges.

4

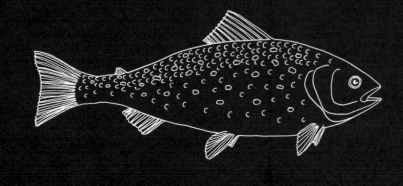

LILLIAN GISH

Pubs and beer have a wonderfully long and close relationship with London's East End, home of colourful and creative Cockney rhyming slang. 'Lillian Gish' is rhyming slang for fish — Lillian Gish having been the first big star of the silent screen. Poetic licence extends to using this slang for all seafood. I'm liking it. It's a very colourful chapter title, with an air of glamour, too. And seafood can be glamorous.

Beer and seafood are like peaches and cream. Insert multiple beer commercial superlatives here: cool, ice-cold, crisp and fresh; carbonated and fizzy; refreshing to the palate... just don't allow the beer to overpower the delicate flavour of the seafood. Lagers and pilseners are the go with addictively salty fried food, refreshingly chilled to abate the heat of fresh, dried or smoked chilli (of which seafood is very fond). Wheat beers and some dark ales with malty, caramel-like tones can also apply for a spot in this chapter. Go on then, get yourself a pig's ear (beer)!

STEAMED WHOLE FISH WITH GINGER AND SPRING ONIONS

This is a very pure recipe in that it pays deep respect to fresh ingredients, which is often a feature of Cantonese cooking. In choosing a beer, consider that fresh, white fish from the sea has a delicate, sweet flavour that could easily be overpowered by anything too strong, so avoid a dark, hearty brew. Besides the obvious choice of lager, some Belgian wheat beers, flavoured with coriander (cilantro) or orange, would sit very nicely with this dish.

1 **whole snapper** > *about 1 kg (2 lb 4 oz)* > *cleaned and gutted*

1 tablespoon **Chinese rice wine**

6 **spring onions** *(scallions)* > *white and green parts finely shredded* > *kept separate*

5 cm *(2 inch)* chunk **fresh ginger** > *peeled and cut into thick matchsticks*

2 tablespoons **light soy sauce**

2 tablespoons **chicken stock**

1 teaspoon **sugar**

60 ml *(2 fl oz/¼ cup)* **peanut oil**

steamed rice and coriander *(cilantro)* > *to serve*

SERVES **4**

1 ··· Put the fish in a heatproof dish and add the rice wine. Set aside for 10 minutes to marinate. Strew the spring onion whites and ginger over the fish. Combine the soy sauce, stock and sugar, then pour over the fish.

2 ··· Sit the dish in a large bamboo steamer basket set over boiling water. Cover and steam for 12–15 minutes, or until the fish is cooked through; it will have white flakes of flesh that easily pull away from the bones. Scatter the green spring onion bits over the fish.

3 ··· Heat the peanut oil in a small saucepan until smoking hot, then pour the hot oil all over the fish. Serve with steamed rice and coriander.

MOROCCAN PAN-FRIED PRAWNS

F+B

LILLIAN GISH

Essaouira is a pretty-as-a-picture, seaside walled city in Morocco. And the seafood is fresh as fresh can be. This recipe is a little similar to the Spanish tapas favourite, garlic prawns — a dish in which fresh prawns bubble to pink goodness in a molten-hot vat of olive oil, butter and garlic. Beers are brewed in Morocco, believe it or not. While Casablanca pale lager does not rate highly with connoisseurs, it does have great retro beer labels. Buy a bottle for that alone.

SERVES 4

60 ml *(2 fl oz/¼ cup)* **olive oil**

2 tablespoons **butter**

4 **garlic cloves** > *chopped*

½ teaspoon **chilli powder**

1 teaspoon **sweet paprika**

1 teaspoon **ground cumin**

24 **large prawns** *(shrimp)* > *peeled and deveined* > *tails intact*

small handful **coriander** *(cilantro)* > *roughly chopped*

small handful **flat-leaf** *(Italian)* **parsley** > *roughly chopped*

crusty bread and salad > *to serve*

1 ··· Heat the oil and butter in a large frying pan over medium heat. When the butter is sizzling, add the garlic and stir-fry for 1 minute, or until softened and aromatic.

2 ··· Stir in the chilli powder, paprika and cumin and cook for a few seconds, so the spices are no longer raw.

3 ··· Add the prawns and stir-fry for 2–3 minutes, or until they turn an even pink colour. Stir in the coriander and parsley. Serve with crusty bread and salad.

SQUID IN LOTS OF CHILLI

The quantity of chilli in this Korean seafood favourite is not a mistake; the salty soy and tangy vinegar balance it out. A purist might question the idea of blanching the squid, but I simply cannot get a wok or pan hot enough to cook the squid quickly, which is what it needs to be tender, so this is a practical way to achieve a really delicious result. To go with it, search out some decent South Korean lagers, such as OB and Hite, or settle for a Japanese lager or pilsener.

500 g *(1 lb 2 oz)* **squid tubes**
2 tablespoons **light soy sauce**
1 tablespoon **chilli flakes**
1 tablespoon **sambal** *(see note)* **or chilli paste**
1 tablespoon **Chinese rice wine vinegar**
1 teaspoon **sugar**
60 ml *(2 fl oz/¼ cup)* **light cooking oil**
2 **onions** > *cut into wedges*
1 **green capsicum** *(pepper)* > *cut into thin strips*
3 **spring onions** *(scallions)* > *sliced on an angle*
6 **garlic cloves** > *finely chopped*
1 tablespoon **fresh ginger** > *finely grated*
½ teaspoon **sesame oil**
toasted sesame seeds and steamed white rice > *to serve*

SERVES **4**

1 · · · Cut the squid into pieces about 5 cm (2 inches) long and 1 cm (½ inch) wide. Bring a saucepan of water to the boil. Add the squid and blanch for 1 minute (no longer or it will toughen), using tongs or chopsticks to separate the squid in the boiling water. Drain the squid and tip into a bowl.

2 · · · Mix together the soy sauce, chilli flakes, sambal, vinegar and sugar.

3 · · · Heat the oil in a large frying pan or wok over high heat. When the oil is smoking hot, add the onion and stir-fry for 2–3 minutes, or until it is just turning golden. Add the capsicum and spring onion and stir-fry for a couple of minutes, then stir in the garlic and ginger. Stir-fry for 1 minute, or until the garlic and ginger have softened and are aromatic.

4 · · · Add the soy sauce mixture to the pan and stir. When the sauce starts to boil, stir in the squid, then the sesame oil. Sprinkle with sesame seeds and serve with steamed rice.

NOTE: Sambal is sauce typically made from a variety of chillies and ingredients such as shrimp paste, fish sauce, garlic, ginger, shallot, spring onion (scallion), sugar, lime juice and vinegar. You'll find it in speciality Asian food stores.

FISH BAKED IN CHIPOTLE

*I'm a fan of adobo and there are several versions in this book.
Each has a twist, as adobo is a marinade that's popular all over the world.
The Spanish, and the Portuguese for that matter, combine vinegar, garlic and
spices to braise meat, chicken and seafood. This technique spread to Mexico
and the Philippines, where adobo has national culinary status. Mexican adobo,
like this version, is more spice-laden. A dark ale goes curiously well with this.*

750 g *(1 lb 10 oz)* **firm white fish, such as ling** > *cut into 5 cm (2 inch) chunks*

150 g *(5½ oz/1 cup)* **plain** *(all-purpose)* **flour**

125 ml *(4 fl oz/½ cup)* **light olive oil**

1 **onion** > *finely chopped*

1 **garlic clove** > *finely chopped*

1 teaspoon **ground cumin**

1 teaspoon **dried oregano**

½ teaspoon **ground cinnamon**

2 **cloves**

1 **chipotle chilli** > *in adobo sauce* > *finely chopped*

400 g *(14 oz)* tin **chopped tomatoes**

coriander *(cilantro)* **sprigs and lime wedges** > *to serve*

SERVES **4**

1 ··· Preheat the oven to 180°C (350°F). Season the fish pieces with sea salt
and freshly ground black pepper. Toss the fish in the flour to lightly and evenly
coat it all over.

2 ··· Heat the oil in a frying pan over high heat. Cook the fish in batches,
for about 2–3 minutes, turning the fish around in the oil, until all the bits
are evenly golden. Place the fish in a ceramic baking dish.

3 ··· Pour off all but 2 tablespoons of the oil from the pan. Add the onion and
garlic and stir-fry for a few minutes, or until softened. Stir in the cumin, oregano,
cinnamon and cloves, then cook for just 1 minute, or until aromatic. Add the
chipotle and tomatoes, stir and simmer for 10 minutes, or until all the liquid
has reduced slightly.

4 ··· Pour the sauce over the fish. Transfer to the oven and bake, uncovered,
for 10 minutes, or until the fish is just cooked through. Sprinkle with coriander
and serve with lime wedges.

F + B

BEER

There are quite a few Mexican <u>cerveza</u> (beers) around these days, and I'm sure many of us would know a few off the top of our heads. Most of the ubiquitous Mexican beers are pale, crisp lagers, although Mexico also produces its fair share of German-style <u>dunkel</u> (dark) lagers. With caramel notes and a hint of chocolate, a dark Mexican lager would be a good match for dishes featuring aromatic spices and chipotle or smoked chilli flavours.

BAKED PRAWNS WITH FETA

It's not often you see seafood and cheese together, but this number has 'Mediterranean' written all over it, with its combination of seafood, herbs, tomatoes and feta. It can be tricky matching beer with acidic tomato-based dishes. A lighter lager might get lost, and anything too crisp just doesn't seem to work. With the addition of sweet, earthy herbs such as dill and oregano, a not too cold, full-bodied, malty and fruity ale would sit nicely with this classic Greek dish.

80 ml *(2½ fl oz/⅓ cup)* **olive oil**

1 **red onion** > *thinly sliced*

65 g *(2¼ oz/1 cup)* **spring onions** *(scallions)* > *thinly sliced*

2 **garlic cloves** > *finely chopped*

large handful **flat-leaf** *(Italian)* **parsley** > *chopped*

small handful **dill** > *chopped*

½ teaspoon **dried oregano**

125 ml *(4 fl oz/½ cup)* **white wine**

400 g *(14 oz)* tin **chopped tomatoes**

2 tablespoons **tomato paste** *(concentrated purée)*

12 **large raw prawns** *(shrimp)* > *peeled and deveined* > *tails intact*

150 g *(5½ oz)* **Greek feta cheese** > *roughly crumbled*

extra chopped dill, lemon wedges and crusty bread > *to serve*

SERVES **2**

1 · · · Preheat the oven to 180°C (350°F). Heat the oil in an ovenproof frying pan over medium–high heat. Cook the onion, spring onion and garlic for 8–10 minutes, or until the onion has softened.

2 · · · Add the parsley, dill, oregano and white wine and cook for a few more minutes, until the wine has simmered down by half. Stir in the tomatoes, tomato paste and 125 ml (4 fl oz/½ cup) water and simmer for 10 minutes, or until the liquid has thickened.

3 · · · If you don't have an ovenproof frying pan, pour the sauce into a baking dish. Lay the prawns on top of the sauce and toss the feta over the prawns.

4 · · · Transfer to the oven and bake for 10 minutes, or until the prawns are pink and cooked through, and the feta has softened and melted into the sauce.

5 · · · Serve warm, sprinkled with a little extra dill, with some lemon wedges and crusty bread on the side.

BAKED PRAWNS WITH FETA

LEBANESE FISH

F
+
B

LILLIAN GISH

The tahini sauce here is the Lebanese version of a tarator, a sauce from many areas of the Middle East. Addictive and versatile, it's an exotic staple to keep in the fridge; I've eaten it for breakfast spread on toast, topped with tomato and avocado. Here it's used as a delicious base on which to bake the fish. Traditionally, the fish is smothered in the tahini first, but I prefer the look of it this way. I'd be inclined to drink a pilsener, such as Lebanon's popular Almaza, or a wheat beer with this.

135 g *(4¾ oz/½ cup)* **tahini**

2–3 tablespoons **lemon juice**

½ teaspoon **sea salt**

500 g *(1 lb 2 oz)* **white fish fillets**

ground white pepper > *for seasoning*

60 ml *(2 fl oz/¼ cup)* **light olive oil**

6 **garlic cloves** > *finely chopped*

3 tablespoons **coriander** *(cilantro)* > *finely chopped*

½ teaspoon **chilli flakes**

40 g *(1½ oz/¼ cup)* **pine nuts**

warm flatbread and tabouleh > *to serve*

SERVES 4

1 ··· In a small bowl, whisk the tahini with the lemon juice and salt. Whisk in 60 ml (2 fl oz/¼ cup) cold water to make a smooth sauce. This sauce, known as tarator, can be kept in an airtight container in the fridge for up to 1 week.

2 ··· Preheat the oven to 180°C (350°F). Spoon the tarator into a ceramic baking dish. Season the fish with a little sea salt and ground white pepper.

3 ··· Heat the oil in a frying pan or wok over high heat. When the oil is shimmering, lower the fish into the oil, in batches if need be, and cook for just 1 minute on each side, or until golden. Place the fish on top of the tarator sauce.

4 ··· Pour off all but 1–2 tablespoons of oil from the pan. Return the pan to the heat. Add the garlic and coriander and stir-fry for just a few seconds to soften the garlic. Remove from the heat and stir the chilli flakes and pine nuts through. Pour the mixture over the fish.

5 ··· Transfer to the oven and bake for 10–15 minutes, or until the pine nuts are golden and the fish is just cooked through. Serve with flatbread and tabouleh.

CARAMEL CLAYPOT FISH

F+B

LILLIAN GISH

This is a great recipe to have up your sleeve. The caramel isn't really caramel in the dessert sense — more a thin, well-balanced, sweet, salty, savoury sauce that can be used with chicken and pork, too. Enjoy this with '33' Export or Saigon lager, the latter being a pale, grainy lager with a hint of lemongrass. You will find both these beers and Hanoi, another Vietnamese lager, at your local bottle shop.

SERVES 4

1 tablespoon **white sugar**

60 ml *(2 fl oz/¼ cup)* **vegetable oil**

2 **garlic cloves** > *finely chopped*

small handful **spring onions** *(scallions)* > *thinly sliced*

400 g *(14 oz)* **firm white fish fillets** > *such as red snapper*

2 tablespoons **fish sauce**

¼ teaspoon **ground white pepper**

steamed jasmine rice > *to serve*

1 · · · Put the sugar in a small saucepan or frying pan and cook over high heat, without stirring. Shake the pan from time to time so any bits of sugar on the sides of the pan are incorporated.

2 · · · When the sugar starts to melt and turn a pale tea colour, use a pair of chopsticks or a wooden spoon to stir until the sugar is coffee-coloured. Slowly add 65 ml (2 fl oz) water, stirring as you do. The caramel will splutter and sizzle, but will settle down as all the water is added. Keep stirring to dissolve any toffee-like bits, until the caramel is thin and the colour of tea. Remove from the heat.

3 · · · Heat the oil in a seasoned clay pot, or in flameproof heavy-based casserole dish. Add the garlic and spring onion and stir-fry for 10 seconds, or until softened.

4 · · · Add the fish pieces and stir. Add the caramel sauce, turning the fish pieces over in the pot. Add the fish sauce and pepper and shake the pan to remove any stuck-on bits of fish. Cover and cook for 5 minutes, then serve with steamed jasmine rice.

Sitting in a cafe on just about any street corner in Hanoi, you can enjoy the local brew, <u>bia hoi</u>, which roughly translates to 'fizzy beer'. It's made daily and delivered to bars and cafes in plastic jugs. It is an egalitarian beer enjoyed by the new-rich as well as the working class, but unfortunately it is a treat you won't be able to enjoy outside Vietnam. The closest you'll find to a <u>bia hoi</u> is a light-alcohol, American-style lager.

MOQUECA (BRAZILIAN FISH STEW)

This is a very old, unbastardised recipe. Some might call it Brazil's version of a curry, similar to a Thai coconut milk-based curry, but it is so much more delicate and subtle in flavour. I would say it's more like a fish stew. This simple recipe requires few ingredients and lacks anything similar to a curry paste, so do make sure all your ingredients are very fresh. A lager goes great with this one.

400 g *(14 oz)* **firm, fresh white fish fillets** > *cut into large chunks*

12 **large raw prawns** *(shrimp)* > *peeled and deveined* > *tails intact*

60 ml *(2 fl oz/¼ cup)* **lime juice**

60 ml *(2 fl oz/¼ cup)* **olive oil**

1 **onion** > *cut into thin wedges*

6 **garlic cloves** > *finely chopped*

1 **large red chilli** > *thinly sliced*

1 **small green capsicum** *(pepper)* > *thinly sliced*

400 ml *(14 fl oz)* **coconut milk**

2 **ripe tomatoes** > *chopped*

handful **coriander** *(cilantro)* > *finely chopped*

small handful **Thai basil leaves**

steamed white rice > *to serve*

SERVES 4

1 · · · Put the fish, prawns and lime juice in a bowl with some sea salt and freshly ground black pepper. Use your hands to toss the seafood to coat with the juice.

2 · · · Heat the oil in a frying pan over high heat. Add the onion and stir-fry for 4–5 minutes, or until softened and just starting to turn golden.

3 · · · Add the garlic, chilli and capsicum and stir-fry for 3–4 minutes, or until the onion and capsicum are tender.

4 · · · Stir in the coconut milk and tomatoes and bring to the boil for 8–10 minutes, or until the sauce has thickened and turned from pale to a pinkish-red colour.

5 · · · Tip the seafood mixture into the sauce and gently stir so all the fish and prawns are immersed in the sauce. Reduce the heat to a low simmer, then cover and cook for 5–6 minutes, or until the fish is tender; the fish will take slightly longer to cook through than the prawns.

6 · · · Stir in the coriander and basil. Season to taste and serve with steamed rice.

SAMBAL PRAWNS

What is going on here? The ingredients look like a real hotchpotch. But then again, this is typical of the dynamic and tasty cuisine of Singapore, where lots of seafood, chillies and noodles are combined with truly East-meets-West flavourings. Who would have thought tomato sauce and malt vinegar could be bedfellows with black beans and sesame oil? A golden ale or wheat beer wouldn't go astray.

200 g *(7 oz)* **hokkien** *(egg)* **noodles**

60 ml *(2 fl oz/¼ cup)* **vegetable oil**

100 g *(3½ oz)* **green beans** > *trimmed* > *cut into 3 cm (1¼ inch) lengths*

1 **onion** > *halved* > *cut into wedges*

4 **garlic cloves** > *chopped*

2 cm *(¾ inch)* chunk **fresh ginger** > *peeled and finely chopped*

2 **large red chillies** > *thinly sliced*

2 **spring onions** *(scallions)* > *thinly sliced*

300 g *(10½ oz)* **raw prawns** *(shrimp)* > *deveined* > *unpeeled*

1 tablespoon **black beans** > *mashed*

1 tablespoon **sambal** *(see note, page 179)* **or chilli paste**

2 tablespoons **malt vinegar**

2 tablespoons **tomato sauce**

1 tablespoon **brown sugar**

1 tablespoon **light soy sauce**

½ teaspoon **sesame oil**

SERVES **4**

1 ··· Put the noodles in a bowl and cover with boiling water. Leave for a couple of minutes, or until softened. Drain.

2 ··· Heat the oil in a large heavy-based frying pan over high heat. Add the beans and onion and stir-fry for 8–10 minutes, or until the onion is golden and the beans are tender.

3 ··· Stir through the garlic, ginger, sliced chilli and spring onion and cook for 1 minute, or until aromatic.

4 ··· Add the prawns and stir-fry for 4–5 minutes, or until they turn pink. Add the black beans, sambal, vinegar, tomato sauce, sugar, soy sauce and 125 ml (4 fl oz/½ cup) water. Stir the ingredients, allowing the sauce to boil and thickly coat the prawns.

5 ··· Add the noodles and sesame oil, stirring them in well. Cook for 1–2 minutes, or until the noodles are heated through and are coated in the spicy sauce.

KING PRAWN BURRITO

I stumbled on this recipe by serendipity. I'd been reading about Mexican cooking and I had a bare cupboard. Well, almost bare except for vinegar and dried chillies, and a couple of jalapeño chillies and limes in the fridge and some prawns in the freezer. This was the delicious result. What's Mexican for voilà? A cool, clean lager or two will have your tastebuds dancing.

SERVES 2

2 tablespoons **lime juice**

½ teaspoon **sea salt**

¼ teaspoon **freshly ground black pepper**

16 large **raw prawns** *(shrimp) > peeled and deveined*

60 ml *(2 fl oz/¼ cup)* **olive oil**

4 **soft tacos**

½ **iceberg lettuce** *> shredded*

coriander *(cilantro)* **sprigs and thinly sliced onion** *> to serve*

HOT SALSA

250 ml *(9 fl oz/1 cup)* **white wine vinegar**

6 **large dried red chillies** *> about 5 cm (2 inches) long*

1 **onion** *> chopped*

6 **garlic cloves** *> chopped*

2 **fresh jalapeño chillies** *> seeded and chopped*

½ teaspoon **sea salt**

1 · · · Combine the lime juice, salt, pepper and prawns in a bowl, tossing the prawns around to coat them in the marinade.

2 · · · To make the salsa, put the vinegar and chillies in a small saucepan. Bring to the boil, then leave to cool for a few minutes. When cool enough to handle, pick out the chillies, reserving the vinegar. Pick the ends off the chillies and squeeze out as many seeds as you can. Roughly chop the chillies and place in a small food processor or spice mill with the onion, garlic, jalapeño chillies and salt. With the motor running, add the vinegar to make a rough-looking salsa.

3 · · · Heat the oil in a frying pan over high heat and cook the prawns for just a couple of minutes on each side, or until they turn pink. Remove to a plate. Add the salsa to the pan and cook for 3–4 minutes. You want the raw ingredients to cook and combine, but still retain a fresh bite.

4 · · · Return the prawns to the pan and stir to warm through. Serve the prawns in soft tacos with the lettuce, coriander and onion.

PRAWN KORMA

A korma sauce is mildly spiced, yet wonderfully fragrant. It is nutty and rich from cashews and cream, with the inclusion of yoghurt balancing out all the creamy richness. Chicken is pretty good in a korma, but prawns or firm white fish are my preference. With a quintessential Indian name, Bangalore-brewed Taj Mahal beer is more like an American-style beer, but full bodied with hops and malt. It's a nice choice with most Indian flavours.

4 **garlic cloves** > *chopped*

1 tablespoon **fresh ginger** > *peeled and grated*

1 **large onion** > *chopped*

80 g *(2¾ oz/½ cup)* **salted cashews** > *plus extra* > *to serve*

2 tablespoons **vegetable oil**

50 g *(1¾ oz)* **butter**

1 teaspoon **cumin seeds**

1 teaspoon **ground coriander**

½ teaspoon **chilli powder**

½ teaspoon **ground turmeric**

½ teaspoon **sea salt**

1 tablespoon **tomato paste** *(concentrated purée)*

125 g (4½ oz/½ cup) **plain yoghurt**

250 ml *(9 fl oz/1 cup)* **thick** *(double/heavy)* **cream**

20 **large green prawns** *(shrimp)* > *peeled and deveined* > *tails intact*

small handful **roughly chopped coriander** *(cilantro)*

SERVES **4**

1 · · · Put the garlic, ginger, onion, cashews and oil in a food processor and blend to a finely chopped paste.

2 · · · Heat the butter in a heavy-based saucepan over medium–high heat. Add the onion mixture and stir-fry for 2–3 minutes, or until golden. Add the cumin, coriander, chilli, turmeric and salt and stir-fry for a few minutes, until aromatic.

3 · · · Stir in the tomato paste. Add 1 tablespoon of the yoghurt and cook for a few seconds, stirring. Repeat with the remaining yoghurt. (Adding the yoghurt gradually will prevent the sauce splitting.) Reduce the heat to medium–low.

4 · · · Add the cream, stirring to remove any bits stuck to the bottom of the pan. Bring the mixture to a low simmer, but do not let the cream boil. Cook for 8–10 minutes, or until the sauce has thickened and the flavour has enriched.

5 · · · Stir in the prawns. Cover and cook for 5 minutes, or until the prawns are cooked through. Stir in the coriander and serve with extra cashews.

FISH CURRY

For all its simplicity, this Southern Indian dish is surprisingly good. Please hunt down fresh curry leaves from an Asian specialty store, where they are often kept in the fridge. While curries often taste better the next day, I've fast-tracked things by cooking the sauce and then setting it aside for a short while for the flavours to develop. And they really do. Then all you do is poach the fish in the sauce (or 'gravy', as they refer to it in India), then sit back and enjoy with a golden ale.

S
E
R
V
E
S

4

60 ml *(2 fl oz/¼ cup)* **vegetable oil**

1 teaspoon **brown mustard seeds**

30–36 **curry leaves** > *left on stem*

4 **red Asian onions or spring onions** *(scallions)* > *finely chopped*

3 **garlic cloves** > *finely chopped*

5 cm *(2 inch)* chunk **fresh ginger** > *peeled and finely chopped*

1 teaspoon **chilli powder**

1 teaspoon **ground coriander**

1 teaspoon **ground turmeric**

1 teaspoon **fenugreek seeds**

½ teaspoon **sea salt**

4 **firm white fish fillets** > *about 200 g (7 oz) each* > *skin on*

steamed basmati rice > *to serve*

1 · · · Heat the oil in a heavy-based frying pan over high heat. Add the mustard seeds, allowing them to pop in the hot oil for a few seconds. Now add the curry leaves, onion, garlic and ginger and stir-fry for a couple of minutes, or until the onion has softened and the mixture is aromatic.

2 · · · Add the chilli powder, coriander, turmeric and fenugreek and stir-fry for no longer than 1 minute. The ground spices will combine to a thick paste and become aromatic. Avoid burning the spices.

3 · · · Stir in 250 ml (9 fl oz/1 cup) water and the salt. Bring to the boil for 2–3 minutes, then reduce the heat and simmer for about 10 minutes. Remove from the heat and set aside for about 1 hour, to allow the flavours to develop.

4 · · · Return the pan to high heat and bring the sauce to the boil. Lay the fish in the pan, skin side down. Reduce the heat to medium, so the sauce comes back to a simmer, spooning some of the sauce over the fish pieces.

5 · · · Cover the pan and cook for 5–6 minutes, or until the fish is just cooked through. Serve with steamed basmati rice.

BLACK PEPPER CRAB

Granted, crabs are funny critters. I am no fan of crab 'meat' in a can, but I'm a huge fan of fresh crab from the seafood market. If you are too, grab whatever crab is local to you. The crab is really a carrier for this drop-dead tasty sauce. This is a real fusion dish: part Chinese, part Indian, part Malaysian. Don't even think of eating this with cutlery; it would be a crime. All you need is some steamed rice and a finger bowl, and maybe a few napkins. And of course a lager.

4 **blue swimmer crabs** > *about 1.5 kg (3 lb 5 oz)*

2 tablespoons **small dried shrimp** > *from Asian food stores*

2 tablespoons **freshly ground black pepper**

½ teaspoon **sea salt**

4 **large garlic cloves** > *finely chopped*

4 **spring onions** *(scallions)* > *finely chopped*

8 **small red chillies** > *finely chopped*

24 **fresh curry leaves**

60 ml *(2 fl oz/¼ cup)* **oyster sauce**

2 tablespoons **dark soy sauce**

55 g *(2 oz/¼ cup)* **sugar**

1 litre *(35 fl oz/4 cups)* **vegetable or canola oil** > *for frying*

80 g *(2¾ oz)* **butter**

steamed basmati rice > *to serve*

SERVES **4**

1 · · · First, prepare the crabs. I find this is best done under cold running water. Working with one crab at a time, hold the front of the crab's head and pull the top of the head off and discard. You will see the gills, called 'dead man's fingers', which are easily removed under the running water. This will also wash away any of the murky bits, leaving the shell, cartilage and the white meat. Now pull off the crab's tail and discard. Shake off the excess water and put the crab on a chopping board.

2 · · · Cut the crab lengthways down the middle so you have two body parts, each with the same number of legs. Now cut each half crossways between the middle two legs. This will give you four parts to each crab, with each part having two legs.

3 · · · Use the back of a cleaver or a rolling pin, or even the bottom of a beer bottle, to crack the larger leg parts in several places. Cracking open the shell allows the cooking flavours to get into the meat. Place all the prepared crab pieces in a large bowl or on a baking tray and store in the fridge until needed.

4 · · · Wrap the dried shrimp in foil. Sit the foil parcel in a small frying pan and cook over high heat, shaking the pan every so often, until you can smell the intense aroma of the shrimp cooking. Remove from the pan using tongs, then open the foil and let the shrimp cool. Tip them into a small food processor or spice mill and grind until finely chopped. Tip them into a bowl and add the pepper, salt, garlic, spring onion, chilli and curry leaves.

5 · · · Combine the oyster sauce, soy sauce and sugar in a small bowl. Set aside.

6 · · · Pour the oil into a wok and heat over high heat. The oil is ready when the surface is shimmering. Don't be tempted to cook all the crab at once — you want it to flash-fry, not stew. Add about one-quarter of the crab pieces and fry for just 2–3 minutes, using metal tongs to turn the crab, until the shells turn pink. Remove to a big bowl or tray. Let the oil reheat after cooking each batch. Repeat with all the crab.

7 · · · Pour off all but a couple of tablespoons of oil from the wok. Add the butter and let it sizzle and melt into the oil. Add the shrimp mixture to the sizzling butter and stir it around for a few seconds until aromatic. Add the crab and cook in the wok for 4–5 minutes, turning the pieces around so they are coated in the peppery aromatics.

8 · · · Add the oyster sauce mixture and stir the crab pieces around to coat in the sauce. Cook for just a couple of minutes so everything is heated through. Serve with basmati rice.

BLACK PEPPER CRAB

MUSSELS WITH FRIES

I like mussels cooked with tomatoes, parsley, coriander (cilantro), beer or wine… but not cream. The chip cooking method may seem a bit left field, but it's fuss free and lets you get on with other things, like having a beer. If that's too much for you, just dunk some bread in the sauce. Try La Chouffe, a bottle-fermented Belgian blonde–style beer with this. Clean and crisp, it has a zippy, fruity taste of orange and coriander that complements the mussel broth and washes the palate clean.

1 kg *(2 lb 4 oz)* **mussels** > *scrubbed > hairy beards removed*

2 tablespoons **unsalted butter**

1 tablespoon **olive oil**

2 **spring onions** *(scallions)* > *chopped*

2 **garlic cloves** > *finely chopped*

½ teaspoon **sea salt**

330 ml *(11¼ fl oz)* **Belgian beer**

small handful **flat-leaf** *(Italian)* **parsley** > *finely chopped*

mayonnaise > *to serve*

SERVES 4

FRIES

1 kg *(2 lb 4 oz)* **desiree potatoes** > *cleaned, skin on > cut into chips 2 cm (¾ inch) wide*

vegetable oil > *for frying*

sea salt > *to serve*

1 · · · Preheat the oven to 160°C (315°F). To make the fries, put the potato chips in a colander and rinse under cold water to remove some of the starch. Tip onto a clean tea towel (dish towel) and pat completely dry. Place in a heavy-based saucepan, then pour enough vegetable oil over to cover. Heat over high heat. Use tongs to separate the chips and move them around in the pan as they slowly start to cook in the oil. When the oil starts to boil, cook for about 5 minutes, or until the fries are golden and crisp.

2 · · · Drain in a colander set over a clean, dry saucepan. Spread the fries on a lined baking tray and bake for 15–20 minutes while you cook the mussels.

3 · · · Discard any broken mussels, or open ones that don't close when tapped on the bench. Heat the butter and oil in a large heavy-based saucepan over high heat. Stir-fry the spring onion and garlic for just 1 minute, or until softened and aromatic. Add the salt and beer and bring to the boil.

4 · · · Add the mussels, stir a few times, then quickly cover the pan. Cook until the mussels have opened, which should only take a few minutes. Discard any unopened mussels, stir in the parsley, and serve with the fries and mayonnaise.

CALAMARI FRITTI

F
+
B

LILLIAN GISH

Ah, the wonders of modern shopping: I came across a local flour company producing '00' flour, and was able to grab some fresh, local squid from my supermarket. After a light coating of flour, the resulting fried squid was crispy, golden and soft as jelly. What a revelation! The rocket and lemon are classic Mediterranean, but you could try a continental flavour shift and serve the squid with good soy sauce and coriander (cilantro). A lager is the go here.

3 **large squid hoods** > *about 500 g (1 lb 2 oz) in total* > *cleaned*

150 g *(5½ oz/1 cup)* **'00' flour**

vegetable oil > *for frying*

wild rocket *(arugula)* **and lemon wedges** > *to serve*

sea salt > *to serve*

SERVES 4

1 · · · Cut each squid hood open, into one large flat piece. Give them a quick rinse under cold water and pat dry. Slice the squid into thin strips, no wider than 1 cm (½ inch). Combine the flour and a little sea salt in a bowl.

2 · · · Pour enough oil into a small saucepan to come about halfway up the side and heat over high heat. You want the oil to be really hot, so the squid flash-fries and cooks in a matter of seconds. The oil is ready when the surface is shimmering.

3 · · · Take several pieces of squid and toss them in the flour to coat all over. Using metal tongs, put the squid in the pan and flash-fry for no more than 10 seconds. It will look a bit like pasta cooking in boiling water. Remove the cooked squid and drain on paper towel. (I actually use an empty cardboard egg carton — I've found it's an ideal way to absorb excess oil.) Cook the remaining squid in batches.

4 · · · Serve the squid on a bed of rocket leaves. The heat of the squid will soften the rocket and add a light peppery flavour. Serve with lemon wedges and a scattering of sea salt.

5

A BEER'S BEST FRIEND

So, you crave rice, pasta or bread after a few beers? You're not Robinson Crusoe there. Rice and noodles are our carbohydrate staples (along with bread, of course), but never forget that beer came before bread!

Call me old fashioned, but I go against the current trend and find it really difficult to eat and enjoy a meal without noodles, rice, pasta or bread. These are a beer's best friend, either eaten with beer, or the day after the night before. These chameleon carrier foods know no bounds.

Spiced-up and savoury, comforting and hunger-sating, the dishes in this chapter will go with any complex brew, robust or light, across the beer spectrum from lager to stout. A beer or two may lend insight into some of these crazy-sounding recipes... Ants climbing trees and dirty rice. What the what?

ANTS CLIMBING TREES

You have to love this intriguing title. Although it evokes an image not necessarily conducive to eating, it is so Chinese to give something a name that elevates it to another level. The key to this simple stir-fry is the noodle. You must use vermicelli made from bean starch: rice noodles just won't work. This dish is so Chinese it begs for a cold Tsingtao, which is so clean, light and drinkable thanks to the inclusion of rice, which is also used in popular Western beers such as Budweiser and Coors.

SERVES **4**

300 g *(10½ oz)* **minced** *(ground)* **pork**

1 tablespoon **light soy sauce**

2 tablespoons **Chinese rice wine**

1 tablespoon **sesame oil**

1 tablespoon **white sugar**

½ teaspoon **sea salt**

2 teaspoons **cornflour** *(cornstarch)*

100 g *(3½ oz)* **bean thread vermicelli noodles**

250 ml *(9 fl oz/1 cup)* **chicken stock**

1 tablespoon **dark soy sauce**

2 tablespoons **light peanut oil**

1 **small red chilli** > *finely chopped*

3 tablespoons **spring onion** *(scallion)* > *thinly sliced*

1 tablespoon **Chinese chilli bean sauce**

1 · · · Combine the pork, light soy sauce, rice wine, sesame oil, sugar and sea salt in a bowl. Add 1 teaspoon of the cornflour. Using your hands, rub the marinade all over the meat. Set aside for 30 minutes in the fridge.

2 · · · Put the noodles in a bowl and cover with hot water. Leave to soften for about 10 minutes, then drain. Combine the stock, dark soy sauce and remaining 1 teaspoon of cornflour in a bowl, stirring until smooth; set aside.

3 · · · Heat the peanut oil in a wok over high heat and swirl the wok around to coat in the oil. Add the chilli and half the spring onion and stir-fry for just a few seconds, until just softened. Add the pork and stir-fry for 4–5 minutes, using a wok spatula or wooden spoon to break the meat up into smaller pieces.

4 · · · Add the chilli bean sauce and stir-fry for a couple of minutes, so the juices in the wok turn a fiery red.

5 · · · Stir the noodles though, then add the stock mixture. Stir-fry for 1 minute. Allow the sauce to boil until it thickly coats the noodles and meat. Serve scattered with the remaining spring onion.

DUCK AND EGG FRIED RICE

I'm partial to both duck and rice. Separate is fine, but together is better. You can use a roasted duck from a Chinese butcher, which you'll see hanging in the shop window alongside other treats such as barbecued pork and soy-braised chickens. I recently found large supermarket chains are selling Peking duck 'kits' and cryo-packed Chinese roast duck. If you see these, grab two roasted duck Marylands. And a few dark ales to enjoy with them.

2 **Chinese roasted duck leg quarters**

1 tablespoon **light soy sauce**

1 tablespoon **Chinese rice wine**

½ teaspoon **sugar**

60 ml *(2 fl oz/¼ cup)* **vegetable oil**

2 **eggs** > *beaten*

1 teaspoon **sesame oil**

2 **garlic cloves** > *chopped*

1 teaspoon **fresh ginger** > *peeled and finely grated*

1 **small red chilli** > *finely chopped*

3 tablespoons **spring onion** *(scallion)* > *white part thinly sliced*

550 g *(1 lb 4 oz/3 cups)* **steamed jasmine rice**

80 g *(2¾ oz/½ cup)* **frozen peas** > *thawed*

ground white pepper and thinly sliced spring onion *(scallion)* **greens** > *to serve*

SERVES 4

1 · · · Pull the meat and skin from the duck, keeping the skin on the meat; discard the bones. Finely slice the meat and set aside. Combine the soy sauce, rice wine and sugar in a small bowl.

2 · · · Heat half the vegetable oil in a wok or large frying pan over high heat, swirling the pan around to coat in the oil. Add the egg and leave to cook without stirring, until the edges start to puff up like an omelette. Use a wooden spoon to stir the egg from the outside to the centre of the pan, and repeat until the egg is just set but still wobbly. Slide the egg onto a chopping board, chop and set aside.

3 · · · Heat the sesame oil and remaining vegetable oil in the wok over high heat. Add the garlic, ginger, chilli and spring onion and stir-fry for 1 minute, or until softened and fragrant. Add the duck and stir-fry for a couple of minutes to heat the duck through.

4 · · · Add the rice and stir-fry for 2–3 minutes. Add the soy sauce mixture, pouring it in around the side of the wok, and stirring it in. Gently stir the peas and egg through, without breaking the egg up too much. Serve sprinkled with white pepper and scattered with green spring onion slices.

SINGAPORE NOODLES

There's some classic and tasty fusion going on here. Chinese flavours and cooking techniques combine with Indian curry powder to produce a really tasty and healthy meal. (I say healthy without thinking about it too much — this dish is riddled with vegetables and also ticks the box for low carbs.) Singapore's Tiger beer is typical of many Asian lagers, being crisp, refreshing and well hopped. It's perfect for most noodle dishes and fried foods with Asian flavours.

SERVES 4

½ **barbecued chicken**

125 g *(4½ oz)* **rice vermicelli**

60 ml *(2 fl oz/¼ cup)* **vegetable oil**

8 **large raw prawns** *(shrimp)* > *peeled and deveined* > *tails intact*

1 **large onion** > *halved* > *cut into wedges*

3 **garlic cloves** > *finely chopped*

5 cm *(2 inch)* chunk **fresh ginger** > *peeled and finely chopped*

1 **small carrot** > *cut into thin matchsticks*

½ **red capsicum** *(pepper)* > *thinly sliced*

45 g *(1½ oz/1 cup)* **Chinese cabbage** > *finely shredded*

large handful **bean sprouts** > *trimmed*

1 tablespoon **mild curry powder**

2 tablespoons **soy sauce**

2 tablespoons **Chinese rice wine**

1 · · · Remove the skin from the chicken and slice it thinly. Tear the meat into thin shreds and place in a bowl with the skin. Refrigerate until needed.

2 · · · Put the noodles in a heatproof bowl and cover with boiling water. Stir the noodles around to separate them, then leave for 5 minutes. Rinse under cold water and leave in a colander to drain well.

3 · · · Heat the oil in a wok over high heat, swirling the wok to coat in the oil. Add the prawns and stir-fry for just 1 minute, until pink. Remove from the wok.

4 · · · Allow the oil to reheat, then stir-fry the onion for 2–3 minutes, or until golden. Add the garlic and ginger and stir-fry for a few seconds, until aromatic.

5 · · · Add the carrot and capsicum and stir-fry for 1 minute. Add the cabbage and bean sprouts and stir-fry for 1–2 minutes, or until the cabbage is tender. Sprinkle the curry powder over and stir until the curry powder is aromatic.

6 · · · Add the noodles to the wok, separating any clumps using tongs. Return the prawns to the wok with the chicken, soy sauce and rice wine. Stir-fry for 2–3 minutes, or until the noodles are no longer white. Serve.

Lagers often have the addition of cereals such as corn, barley and rice. Pale, light-bodied, less bitter and less malty than other beers of the day, lagers became popular in America following Prohibition and World War II. Many Asian breweries also started up in the 1920s and '30s, many of them set up by expat Europeans in the Far East who were missing their beers.

CHICKEN RICE

Also known as arroz con pollo, this is paella for beginners. It's a wonderfully fragrant and easy rice dish to have in your repertoire, with many of the ingredients being kitchen staples — just pick up a ready-cooked roast chicken on the way home from work. The serving accompaniments are optional, but well worth including. Your glass of golden ale will taste all the finer for it.

60 ml *(2 fl oz/¼ cup)* **light olive oil**

2 **red onions** > *sliced into thin wedges*

1 **garlic clove** > *finely chopped*

1 **fresh jalapeño chilli** > *seeded and chopped*

350 g *(12 oz/2 cups)* **shredded barbecued chicken meat and skin**

1 teaspoon **ground cumin**

½ teaspoon **ground cinnamon**

6–8 **saffron threads**

440 g *(15½ oz/2 cups)* **short-grain white rice**

2 **piquillo peppers** > *thinly sliced*

1 litre *(35 fl oz/4 cups)* **chicken stock**

pickled jalapeño chillies and sour cream > *to serve*

SERVES **4**

1 · · · Heat the oil in a saucepan over high heat. Cook the onion for 4–5 minutes, or until softened. Add the garlic and chilli and cook for just 1 minute.

2 · · · Stir the chicken, cumin, cinnamon and saffron through. Add the rice and piquillo peppers. Stir the rice through all the other ingredients and cook for a couple of minutes, or until the rice is nutty and aromatic.

3 · · · Add the stock and bring to the boil without stirring the mixture, but giving the pan a shake to settle everything. Reduce the heat to low, cover and cook for 25 minutes, or until the rice is cooked through.

4 · · · Serve with pickled jalapeño chillies and sour cream.

TOMATO RICE

*The inclusion of butter may seem out of keeping in this dish, but I'm
thinking it's here because the French colonials might have had a say in
this Vietnamese classic. So easy, so very more-ish and so delicious,
tomato rice would traditionally be served with crispy chicken, a fried pork
chop or Shaking beef (see page 141). Enjoy with a refreshing lager.*

300 g *(10½ oz/1½ cups)* **jasmine rice**

60 g *(2¼ oz)* **butter**

2 **garlic cloves** > *finely chopped*

2 tablespoons **tomato paste** *(concentrated purée)*

2 teaspoons **light soy sauce**

¼ teaspoon **ground white pepper**

SERVES 4

1 · · · **Wash the rice in cold water until the water is no longer cloudy. Put the rice
in a saucepan with 750 ml (26 fl oz/3 cups) cold water and place over high heat.
When the water is boiling rapidly, reduce the heat to low, then cover and cook
for 20 minutes. Tip the rice onto a large plate, spreading it out. Refrigerate until
cold; this can also be done overnight.**

2 · · · **Heat a wok or non-stick frying pan over high heat. Add the butter. When it
has melted and is sizzling, add the garlic and cook for just a few seconds to
soften the rawness of the garlic and flavour the butter.**

3 · · · **Add the rice and stir-fry for 1 minute to combine with the garlic butter.
Add the tomato paste and stir-fry for 2–3 minutes. Stir the soy sauce and white
pepper through. Serve hot.**

DIRTY RICE

This has all the hallmarks of southern American cookery: sausage, chicken livers, cayenne pepper and green capsicums (peppers), with influences from France, Africa and the Caribbean. But I just love this name. Doesn't it just say: I taste so good, you can call me whatever you darned well like? I'm dirty, easy and tasty. Enough said. Drink a pilsener with this — a deep-flavoured beer sits nicely with these flavours from the Deep South.

SERVES 4

300 g *(10½ oz/1½ cups)* **basmati rice**

1 tablespoon **light olive oil**

250 g *(9 oz)* **Italian pork and garlic sausages** > *casing removed*

100 g *(3½ oz)* **chicken livers** > *cleaned and roughly chopped*

1 **onion** > *chopped*

1 **garlic clove** > *chopped*

¼ teaspoon **cayenne pepper**

1 **large green chilli** > *thinly sliced*

1 **celery stalk** > *diced*

1 **small green capsicum** *(pepper)* > *diced*

375 ml *(13 fl oz/1½ cups)* **chicken stock**

small handful **flat-leaf** *(Italian)* **parsley** > *chopped*

2 **spring onions** *(scallions)* > *thinly sliced*

hot sauce > *to serve*

1 · · · Cook the rice in lightly salted boiling water for 8 minutes. Rinse under cold water and leave in a colander to drain.

2 · · · Heat the oil in a heavy-based saucepan over high heat. Add the sausage and liver and stir-fry for 2–3 minutes, breaking up any larger sausage pieces. Leave the meat to cook in the pan for a couple of minutes, so it really develops a golden crust, which will give the cooked dish a 'dirty' look.

3 · · · Add the onion, garlic, cayenne pepper, chilli, celery and capsicum. Stir-fry for 2–3 minutes, or until the vegetables have softened.

4 · · · Pour in 125 ml (4 fl oz/½ cup) of the stock, stirring to remove any bits stuck to the bottom of the pan.

5 · · · Add the rice, parsley, spring onion and the remaining stock. Stir, then cover with a tight-fitting lid and cook for 5 minutes. Fluff up the rice using a large spoon, then serve with hot sauce on the side.

CHAR KWAY TEOW

This always reminds me of fast-food courts in Asian shopping centres, where the food is often so good that it's hard to settle on a vendor. I usually go to the one that sells the best won ton noodle soup or this dish, char kway teow — it's hard to go wrong. But I did discover, cooking this at home, that you do need one vital ingredient to make it work well: heat. Fiery heat. My electric hob just didn't cut it, and the ingredients ended up stewing rather than flash-charring to a smoky flecked goodness. So, if you have an electric hob, avoid the wok and opt for a large, flat frying pan. Asian rice and noodle dishes often have lots of vegetables, but are also high in fat, which is why they taste so good. Hawker food stalls in Singapore and Malaysia are popular with locals and tourists alike, and their offerings are best enjoyed with a local lager.

2 **Chinese sausages** *(lap cheong)*

400 g *(14 oz)* **fresh flat rice noodles**

1 tablespoon **Chinese chilli sauce**

1 tablespoon **light soy sauce**

1 tablespoon **dark soy sauce**

60 ml *(2 fl oz/¼ cup)* **vegetable oil**

250 g *(9 oz)* **small raw prawns** *(shrimp) > peeled and deveined > tails intact*

3 **garlic cloves** *> chopped*

¼ teaspoon **ground white pepper**

2 **eggs** *> lightly beaten*

large handful **garlic chives** *> cut into short lengths*

large handful **bean sprouts** *> trimmed*

SERVES 4

1 · · · Put the sausages in a heatproof bowl and cover with boiling water. Leave for 10 minutes, then drain. When cool enough to handle, cut the sausages into thin slices. Place in a bowl and set aside.

2 · · · Place the noodles in a colander. Run some warm water over them, gently separating the noodles using your hands. Leave in the colander to drain.

3 · · · In a bowl, mix together the chilli sauce, light soy and dark soy sauces. Set aside.

4 · · · Heat the oil in a wok over high heat, swirling the wok around to coat it in the oil. Add the Chinese sausage and stir-fry for 1 minute. Now add the prawns and garlic and stir-fry for 1 minute, or until the prawns have just turned pink.

5 · · · Add the noodles, the soy sauce mixture and white pepper. Stir-fry for 2–3 minutes, or until the noodles are well coated and caramel brown.

6 · · · Clear some space in the bottom of the wok. Add the beaten eggs and leave to cook for 1 minute, or until the egg just starts to set around the edge.

7 · · · Fold the egg through the noodles. Add the garlic chives and bean sprouts and stir-fry just until they have wilted. Serve hot.

CHAR KWAY TEOW

BEANS AND RICE

This is a very down-home recipe, and a little different from the Louisiana classic red beans and rice, which has more sauce and includes meat — usually ham or sausage. A bowl of this would do nicely as a simple meal, or you could serve it with some spicy grilled fish or chicken. A dark or golden ale would go down just fine with this.

SERVES **2**

2 tablespoons **olive oil**

1 **onion** > *finely chopped*

1 **garlic clove** > *chopped*

1 **green capsicum** *(pepper)* > *diced*

1 **jalapeño chilli** > *seeded and chopped*

200 g *(7 oz/1 cup)* **long-grain white rice**

1 teaspoon **dried oregano**

1 teaspoon **ground cumin**

2 teaspoons **smoked paprika**

2 tablespoons **tomato paste** *(concentrated purée)*

400 g *(14 oz)* tin **borlotti beans** > *rinsed and well drained*

500 ml *(17 fl oz/2 cups)* **chicken stock**

small handful **coriander** *(cilantro)* **leaves** > *chopped*

lime wedges > *to serve*

1 · · · Heat the oil in a heavy-based saucepan over high heat. Add the onion, garlic, capsicum and chilli and stir-fry for 1 minute, or until softened.

2 · · · Add the rice and stir gently. Sprinkle with the oregano, cumin, paprika and some sea salt and freshly ground black pepper. Stir for 1 minute, or until the raw spices are cooked and aromatic.

3 · · · Add the beans and stock, stirring well to remove any bits stuck to the bottom of the pan. Bring to the boil, then reduce the heat to low. Cover with a tight-fitting lid and cook for 20 minutes.

4 · · · Remove from the heat. Fluff the rice with a fork, then cover and leave for another 5 minutes. Stir the coriander through and serve with lime wedges.

SESAME AND GARLIC CHIVE EGG NOODLES

When you open a bag of fresh egg noodles, the first thing you notice is their fresh, dough-like smell. They're often coated in a dusting of flour to stop them sticking together; parboiling them will remove the starch, but always use a big pot, or the noodles won't separate properly and the flour will bind them together into a gloopy, clumpy mess. Drink tea with this, of course, and serve with a hot chilli sauce. The two yum cha essentials: chilli and tea... or you could opt for a lager instead.

300 g *(10½ oz)* **fresh soft thin egg noodles**

60 ml *(2 fl oz/¼ cup)* **vegetable oil**

1 tablespoon **sesame oil**

125 g *(4½ oz/2 cups)* **garlic chives** > *cut into 3 cm (1¼ inch) lengths*

1 tablespoon **fresh ginger** > *finely grated*

100 g *(3½ oz)* **bean sprouts** > *trimmed*

2 tablespoons **light soy sauce**

1 tablespoon **dark soy sauce**

toasted sesame seeds and sriracha sauce > *to serve*

SERVES **2**

1 · · · Bring a large saucepan of water to the boil. Before adding the noodles, gently pull them apart; being fresh, they might tend to clump together.

2 · · · Add the noodles to the pan and use a large wooden spoon or tongs to gently stir and separate them. The water will turn cloudy. Cook the noodles for no more than 2–3 minutes, or until they start to float to the top. Drain well, then tip the noodles into a clean tea towel (dish towel). Wrap them up in the towel to remove any excess water.

3 · · · Place the noodles in a bowl with half the vegetable oil, using your hands to toss the noodles to coat them in the oil. The noodles can be prepared to this stage in advance and kept covered for 1–2 days in the fridge.

4 · · · Heat the sesame oil and remaining vegetable oil in a wok over high heat. Add the garlic chives and ginger and stir-fry for 1 minute, or until the chives have wilted. Add the bean sprouts and stir-fry until these are just wilted.

5 · · · Add the noodles and stir-fry for 2–3 minutes. Stir in the light soy and dark soy sauces. Tip the noodles into a large bowl. Sprinkle with sesame seeds and serve with sriracha sauce.

THAI FRIED RICE

This is elegant compared to other rice recipes, although it is just as easily slapped up and put together as any other. Jasmine rice is just fragrant enough to get your attention. While many other fried rice recipes contain meat or even prawns, the inclusion of delicate crabmeat here gives this dish a beautiful balance, so typical of Thai cooking. Enjoy it with a wheat beer.

SERVES **4**

200 g *(7 oz/1 cup)* **jasmine rice**

60 ml *(2 fl oz/¼ cup)* **vegetable oil**

2 **garlic cloves** > *finely chopped*

12 **large raw prawns** *(shrimp)* > *peeled and deveined* > *tails intact*

¼ teaspoon **ground white pepper**

¼ teaspoon **white sugar**

1 **egg** > *lightly beaten*

100 g *(3½ oz)* **fresh crabmeat** > *shredded*

60 ml *(2 fl oz/¼ cup)* **light soy sauce**

2 **spring onions** *(scallions)* > *thinly sliced*

lime cheeks, coriander *(cilantro)* **leaves and sliced cucumber** > *to serve*

1. · · · Wash the rice in cold water and repeat until the water is no longer cloudy. (Washing the rice removes excess starch and any impurities.) Drain well, then place in a smallish saucepan with 375 ml (13 fl oz/1½ cups) cold water.

2. · · · Bring to the boil over high heat. When you see small bubbling pockets, reduce the heat to low, cover with a tight-fitting lid and cook for 20 minutes. Tip the cooked rice into a bowl and leave to cool completely.

3. · · · Heat a wok over high heat. Add the oil, swirling it around to coat the wok. Add the garlic and prawns and stir-fry for 1 minute, or until the prawns turn pink and the garlic is golden.

4. · · · Add the rice, white pepper and sugar and stir-fry for a couple of minutes to mix the garlicky oil through the rice.

5. · · · Push the rice to the side of the wok and pour the egg onto the lowest part of the wok. When the egg starts to firm around the edges, stir the egg into the rice. Add the crabmeat, soy sauce and spring onion and stir well. Serve hot, with lime cheeks, coriander and cucumber slices.

Index

Published in 2015 by Murdoch Books,
an imprint of Allen & Unwin

Murdoch Books Australia
83 Alexander Street
Crows Nest NSW 2065
Phone: +61 (0)2 8425 0100
Fax: +61 (0)2 9906 2218
murdochbooks.com.au
info@murdochbooks.com.au

Murdoch Books UK
Erico House, 6th Floor
93–99 Upper Richmond Road
Putney, London SW15 2TG
Phone: +44 (0) 20 8785 5995
murdochbooks.co.uk
info@murdochbooks.co.uk

For Corporate Orders & Custom Publishing contact
Noel Hammond, National Business Development
Manager, Murdoch Books Australia

Publisher: Diana Hill
Editorial Manager: Jane Price
Design Manager: Madeleine Kane
Editors: Katri Hilden, Gordana Trifunovic
Designer & Illustrator: Mash Design
Photographer: Jason Loucas
Stylist: Matt Page
Food Preparation: Wendy Quisumbing
Production Manager: Mary Bjelobrk

Text © Ross Dobson 2015
Design © Murdoch Books 2015
Photography © Jason Loucas 2015

A cataloguing-in-publication entry is available from
the catalogue of the National Library of Australia at
nla.gov.au.

ISBN 978 1 743365489 Australia
ISBN 978 1 743365496 UK

A catalogue record for this book is available from
the British Library.

Colour reproduction by Splitting Image Colour Studio
Pty Ltd, Clayton, Victoria
Printed by 1010 Printing International Ltd, China

IMPORTANT

Those who might be at risk from the effects of
salmonella poisoning (the elderly, pregnant women,
young children and those suffering from immune
deficiency diseases) should consult their doctor with
any concerns about eating raw eggs.

OVEN GUIDE

You may find that cooking times vary, depending on
the oven you are using. For fan-forced ovens, as a
general rule, set the oven temperature to 20°C (35°F)
lower than indicated in the recipe.